UNTIL JUSTICE ROLLS DOWN

UNTIL JUSTICE ROLLS DOWN

The Birmingham Church
Bombing Case

Revised and Updated Edition

FRANK SIKORA

THE UNIVERSITY OF ALABAMA PRESS

TUSCALOOSA

∞

The paper on which this book is printed meets the minimum
requirements of American National Standard for Information Science—
Permanence of Paper for Printed Library Materials, ANSI Z39.48-1984.

Library of Congress Cataloging-in-Publication Data

Sikora, Frank, 1936–
Until justice rolls down : the Birmingham church bombing case /
Frank Sikora.— Rev. ed.
p.   cm. — (Fire ant books)
Includes index.
ISBN-13: 978-0-8173-5268-4 (pbk. : alk. paper)
ISBN-10: 0-8173-5268-6
1. Murder—Alabama—Birmingham. 2. Trials (Murder)—Alabama—
Birmingham. 3. African Americans—Crimes against—Alabama—
Birmingham. 4. Bombings—Alabama—Birmingham. 5. Bombing
investigation—Alabama—Birmingham. 6. Hate crimes—
Alabama—Birmingham. I. Title. II. Series.
HV6534.B5S55 2005
364.152'3'09761781—dc22
2005008452

To John Daniel and Millie

Contents

Preface

Of all the acts of terrorism that marked the civil rights era in the American South, none was more horrifying than the deed that took place in Birmingham, Alabama, on Sunday, September 15, 1963. A bomb exploded that morning at the Sixteenth Street Baptist Church and took the lives of four black girls.

The victims were Denise McNair, age eleven, and Carole Robertson, Addie Mae Collins, and Cynthia Wesley, all fourteen years old. They were at the church that Sunday morning simply to take part in the services and to be ushers. The Ku Klux Klansman who had set the bomb at the church had no idea when it might detonate or who might be injured or killed when it did.

The bombing had occurred at a time when Birmingham, as well as the entire state of Alabama, was in turmoil over school desegregation. Federal courts had ordered a total of twenty-four black children, including five in Birmingham, to be admitted to all-white public schools in Alabama. But the girls killed at the church had not been involved in any of that, nor had they been participants in earlier civil rights marches and demonstrations in Birmingham, which had been led by Dr. Martin Luther King, Jr. They were just four girls, all in the springtime of their lives.

Two hundred FBI agents interviewed hundreds of persons, but the agency could never come up with the evidence and witnesses that officials believed would be needed to prosecute the case. It has been argued that in 1963, when any jury in Alabama would have consisted of twelve white men, no white man or group of white men would be convicted for a racially motivated crime. That point is open for debate; within twenty-six months of the bombing, an all-white jury in Montgomery, in a case presided over by U.S. District Judge Frank M. Johnson, Jr., convicted three klansmen of violating the civil rights of a white woman killed after the Selma-to-Montgomery march. And, four years later, a white jury in a federal court in Mississippi handed down guilty verdicts in the killings of three civil rights workers shot to death in the summer of 1964.

In 1971, the newly elected attorney general of Alabama, William Baxley, fulfilling a pledge made the day of the bombing, began his own probe of the crime. For five years Baxley's staff hammered away at the case, fighting a long battle just to get access to FBI files, which FBI Director J. Edgar Hoover refused to open to Alabama officials. In 1976 Baxley added Bob Eddy to his investigating team and sent him to Birmingham; ten months later, a klansman went before a jury on a charge of murder.

This is the story of the bombing and of Klan terror, and of the investigation into which led to one KKK member being convicted. Moving ahead almost a quarter century to the renewal of the probe, the story continues, involving the FBI, the U.S. attorney's office in Birmingham, the Birmingham Police Department, and the Jefferson County district attorney's staff. The result is two more former KKK members being convicted. Through it all are revelations from FBI files, even tape recordings that apparently in the 1960s were set aside and forgotten about. The three trials are full of dramatic and chilling testimony; the words reveal the stark hatred of some men, men who made the era a dangerous time to live in Birmingham.

The quotations attributed to the persons involved are based on numerous interviews, notes, and, in some cases, tape recordings and transcripts, as well as my own personal observations at the trials. I have expanded the book to include the recent two court cases, and have added a more detailed account of the fifth black child killed that day, Virgil Ware, only thirteen. Now Americans can look back on that ugly day and on those times. And we can only wonder how men could carry out such a cruel and deadly act against children, children who had gone to church on a Sunday morning.

A number of persons have kindly assisted with this book. I especially want to thank Maria Bethune of Birmingham, who typed the original manuscript; Pam Lyons, Marvin Whiting, and Jim Baggett of the Birmingham Public Library; Barbara Niedenthal, Canton, Ohio; and everybody at *The Birmingham News,* especially Ingrid Kindred, Tom Scaritt, Robin DeMonia, and Ron Casey. I also thank, for their advice or encouragement, Jim Jacobson, Sheila Brown, Laurie Orr Dean, James Kennedy, Tom Gordon, Glenn Stephens, Dave Parks, Kent Faulk, Ray Brown, Tom Self, Solomon Crenshaw, Lynn Waddell, Felyicia Pemberton, John Mangels, Frances Spotswood, Voncille Williams, Judy Haise, Carol Nunnelley, Jim Clark, and Rebecca Meigs. Also Sara Jane Tackett, Hubert Grissom, Bob McGregor, Susanna Feld, John Wright, Virginia Hamilton, and Sam Webb, all of Birmingham; Deborah Evans of Camp Hill, Alabama; Tom and Sandra Baxley Taylor, Mobile; Theresa and Dave Compton, Westfield, Indiana; Dan Ross, Malcolm M. Mac-Donald, Linda Sandford, Ellen Stein, Kathleen Domino, Sonia Wilson, Jonathan Lawrence, and Karen Ables of The University of Alabama Press.

Of course, I thank my family, including an assortment of sons, daughters, son-in-law, and grandchildren, all of whom know their last names: Debbie, Michelle, Jan, Victor, Frankie, Terry, Johnny, Dawn, Junior, Kerry, Schanee, Rachel, Ashlee, Tavia, Whitney, Natalie, Ziggy, Scha, and Kristi.

Frank Sikora
Birmingham, Alabama

Addie Mae Collins   Cynthia Wesley

Carole Robertson   Denise McNair

BRING LIGHT TO THIS DARK CITY

1

THE VICTIMS:

Addie Mae Collins   **Cynthia Wesley**

Carole Robertson   **Denise McNair**

Sunday, September 15, 1963. Birmingham, Alabama

When they had first started walking to church that day, their behavior had been proper, befitting young girls on their way to praise the Lord. Addie Mae Collins, age fourteen, often walked the sixteen blocks to the Sixteenth Street Baptist Church with her older sister, Janie, and younger sister, Sarah. But this time, before they had gone more than two blocks, they began playing football, using Addie's purse as the football and giggling and laughing as they ran for passes and dodged about. The route to church was along streets lined with dogwood, oak, and mimosa; the near northwest side of the city was a lower-middle-class, mostly black, neighborhood, where frame houses mingled with small stores and other businesses. A number of girls at the church, including Addie, were to be ushers that day. All were wearing white dresses.

At her house, fourteen-year-old Cynthia Wesley was ready to go out the door with her father, Claude, when she was stopped by her mother. "Young lady, your slip is hanging below your dress," said Gertrude Wesley. "You just don't put your clothes on any way when you're going to church, because you never know how you're coming back." Cynthia had hurriedly made the necessary adjustments before running out the door. She and Mr. Wesley would arrive before the start of Sunday school, 9:30 A.M. Her mother would never see her again.

Meanwhile, Cynthia's closest friend, Carole Robertson, also fourteen, had already arrived at church, driven by her father, Alvin C. Robertson.

The last of the four to arrive was eleven-year-old Carol Denise McNair, who was known to her family and friends as Denise. The day before, Denise, a friend from across the street, Barbara Nunn, and some other children had been playing kickball and a game they called four-square. "It was just a game we made up, I guess," Miss Nunn would say in later times. "Denise was just a kid, just a girl who liked to have fun and play, like all kids. She had a dog she called Whitey. She really loved that dog."

On that Sunday morning Denise was going to go to church early and planned to ride with her father, Chris McNair, a photographer. But he was a member of another church and was running late that morning. So she had told him, "That's okay, Daddy, go ahead." She waited and rode with her mother, saying goodbye to her dog before leaving.

After the hot summer, the day was refreshingly cool, with morning temperatures in the low sixties. Behind a cloud bank, the sun was a silver blur as it edged up above the hump of high hills along the eastern edge of this industrial city of 340,000.

The year 1963 had not been kind to Birmingham; racial discord had projected the city onto the front pages of newspapers around the world, as well as in the eye of TV cameras. City authorities had used dogs and fire hoses to disperse crowds of blacks, and the homes of some black leaders had been bombed.

Martin Luther King, Jr., had announced early in the year that he had selected Birmingham as a target of the South-

4

ern Christian Leadership Conference's effort to overcome racial barriers. He called it the most segregated city in the South.

Birmingham had undergone political upheaval in late 1962 and early 1963, changing its form of government from a three-member commission—one of the commissioners had been Eugene "Bull" Connor—to a mayor-council system. Connor, a hard-line segregationist, had fought the change, but after he failed to block it he entered the race to be the city's new mayor. The election was held March 5; Connor and another candidate, Albert Boutwell, got the most votes but neither received a majority. They faced each other in a runoff on April 2. Boutwell, a soft-spoken racial moderate, won the runoff by more than eight thousand votes, but Connor refused to leave office, filing a court challenge.

Against this backdrop, King came to town. "He was not welcome," recalled *The Birmingham News,* in a commemorative story twenty years later. *The News* had blasted Connor's police department in 1961 for its mishandling of the Freedom Riders who were beaten by klansmen, and in 1963 it also blasted King in an editorial: "His very presence will be upsetting to whites familiar with his Albany [Georgia] record. King has made shocking statements in the past, of personal unwillingness to say in advance whether he would accept court orders—even though he expects whites to do so. His 'non-violent' policy is violated every time he promotes demonstrations or turmoil not related to achievement of justice under the law. . . . He should stay out of Birmingham."

King and the local leader of the Birmingham drive, the Reverend Fred Shuttlesworth, who headed the Alabama Christian Movement, waited until April 3, the day after the runoff, to begin their challenge to the city's laws and customs embracing segregation. On that bright, warm Wednesday, *The News* carried a story on the front page that captured the mood of the day for many people: "This, happily, is a new day for Birmingham. There's a new feeling in the air. There's a new spirit of optimism." The story was signed by the mayor-elect, Albert Boutwell.

On that same day, King and Shuttleworth sent a group of blacks to obtain service at Britling's Restaurant; fourteen were arrested. Simultaneously, other groups went to lunch counters at some of the city's larger department stores— Pizitz, Loveman's, Kress, and Woolworth's. The blacks found "Closed" signs at each of them, but Birmingham's new day had begun.

This was a city where blacks found little in the way of steady employment, other than cleaning up offices or homes, cooking in restaurants, or toiling in the iron and steel foundries; most black professionals were teachers or preachers. There were no black store clerks, secretaries, police officers, librarians, or firefighters. This was the Birmingham that still posted "White only" signs over water fountains and restrooms; black people could not sit at lunch counters or in the main sections of theaters.

King brought his Southern Christian Leadership Conference to Birmingham to marshal a challenge to legal segregation. Although he held rallies at several churches in the black community, the chief rallying spot was the Sixteenth Street Baptist Church, chosen for its size, its history, and its location. The church, a yellow-brown structure built in the Byzantine style, had a membership of more than four hundred, including many prominent black citizens: lawyers, teachers, dentists. It sat cater-corner from Kelly Ingram Park, a one-square-block area of trees and grass that was an ideal place to mobilize an army of marchers and send them down Fifth Avenue to the downtown, just four blocks away. At the church King preached harmony, his words captured by Folkways Records: "I don't like the way Mr. Bull Connor acts, but I love him, because Jesus said love is greater than hate." It was here in Birmingham that the civil rights movement adopted its anthem, "We Shall Overcome."

Marches began in April and resulted in thousands of

arrests. "Never have so many gone to jail in the cause of freedom," said King. Fire hoses and snarling police dogs were used against large groups of spectators who gathered to watch the marches.

On May 9 King and his top aides, Shuttlesworth and Ralph Abernathy, reached an agreement with Birmingham business leaders to desegregate lunch counters, drinking fountains, and restrooms, and to begin hiring blacks as sales clerks. King hailed it as "the most significant victory for justice that we have seen in the Deep South." The agreement was announced on May 10, and on the next day Bull Connor angrily denounced it as King's "lyingest, face-saving" act. That night bombs exploded at the black-owned Gaston Motel and at the home of King's brother, A. D. King. The bombings triggered a riot by twenty-five hundred blacks; fifty persons were injured. President John F. Kennedy sent federal troops to Alabama, staging them at Fort McClellan, near Anniston, and at Maxwell Air Force Base in Montgomery. But the troops never moved into Birmingham, and a strained calm settled over the city. On May 20 Bull Connor, having lost his court challenges of the elections, left office.

The church rallies began to dwindle, and blacks and whites alike tried to return to a more normal life. Then, as autumn approached, the city was again jolted by racial turmoil. Federal judges in Alabama had ordered twenty-four blacks enroll at previously all-white schools. Five of those black students were in Birmingham. Alabama Governor George C. Wallace, who had made his stand in the schoolhouse door at The University of Alabama in June, vowed to fight the desegregation of the state's public schools.

On the night of August 20, 1963, the home of black attorney Arthur Shores was bombed, but no one was hurt. Shores had been involved in the desegregation of The University of Alabama and in efforts to invalidate Birmingham's ordinances maintaining residential segregation. As the opening day of school neared, white resistance

7

mounted. Crowds of whites waving Confederate flags protested desegregation orders and rode motorcades through the city. On the night of September 4 another bomb exploded at Shores's home, this time slightly injuring his wife, Theodora. Blacks reacted in anger, boiling out into Center Street near the Shores home, in the city's near west side. Police hurried to the scene; shots were fired. A black man was shot and killed as he reportedly ran from a house firing a gun. That night, twenty-one persons were injured, including some officers who were struck by bricks, rocks, and bottles.

But on this Sunday morning of September 15, 1963, the din of the desegregation effort had been stilled. At the church, the lesson for the day was "A Love That Forgives."

At 9:10 A.M. church members William and Mamie Grier, both schoolteachers, neared the church in their new blue and white Buick Electra. About two blocks from the church Mrs. Grier pointed at another car and said, "Look at that." What had caught her attention was the Confederate flag that fluttered from the car's radio antenna. Mrs. Grier would later tell the FBI that the car appeared to be a 1955 Chevrolet, greenish in color. It had been driven by a lone white man, she said. Confederate flags had been common on cars during the early 1960s, and many blacks viewed them as a symbol of racial segregation and white supremacy. The Griers had followed the car; it turned on Sixteenth Street, passed the church, then continued on. They watched until it passed from view. Then they turned into the church parking lot. There had been some anxiety among church members because of the rash of bombings in Birmingham in recent weeks, and only the Sunday before, the church secretary, Mary Buycks, had received a phone call from a man who said, "This is the KKK. Your church will be bombed tonight." It had turned out to be a hoax.

2

————
————
————

As the Collins sisters had strolled along playing football, Bennie H. Wilson, deacon in charge of custodial services, was walking up the concrete steps leading to the side entrance of the church. Had he looked under the steps he would have seen it—a box packed with thick sticks of dynamite, each of them wrapped in brownish-green paper. The box had been placed there during the night. But Wilson didn't look, and neither did anyone else. At least a dozen church members would walk up the steps that morning.

Most of the adults gathered upstairs in the main sanctuary, while the children and teenagers went downstairs to the assembly area, a large room with light brown walls that had served the church as a sanctuary until the upstairs was completed in 1911. Some of the Sunday school classes were held in the assembly area, but others were housed in the small rooms that fringed it. In the northeast corner of the basement, almost directly behind the side steps, was the women's lounge.

Ella C. Demand began her class at 9:30; after a discussion of the lesson, some of the teenage girls began talking about their duties as ushers. At about 10:10, Cynthia Wesley and Carole Robertson asked permission to go to the lounge so they could freshen up for the service. They would have to be upstairs by 10:30.

Also at about 10:10 A.M. Maxine McNair and her daughter Denise arrived. Mrs. McNair went to the adult class on the main floor, while Denise hurried down to the small basement room where Mrs. Clevon Phillips was conducting class. A few minutes after she entered the room, Denise raised her hand and asked permission to go to the lounge. The teacher nodded. Out in the assembly area, Denise paused. To her right, about forty feet away, she saw Rosetta Young, one of the sponsors of the youth ushers. Denise ran across the room to her.

"My, don't you look pretty," said Mrs. Young.

The girl smiled. "Thank you, ma'am."

She whirled then, and went to the lounge. Her words to Mrs. Young were probably her last.

In the meantime, the Collins girls were giggling their way along, throwing Addie's purse about and running so hard that they began to perspire.

"This is the best time we've ever had coming to church," said Janie, the oldest at sixteen. Sarah, thirteen, was the youngest; Addie at fourteen. When they finally arrived at the church it was well past 10 A.M. and the Sunday school classes were about over.

"Now come on, y'all," chided Janie. "We can't go into church looking like this. We got all messed up. Come on, we're going down to the lounge to straighten up." They went to the women's lounge in the basement. In a few minutes Janie was ready. "Now y'all hurry and come on up," she called as she left the lounge and went upstairs.

Denise McNair entered the lounge where the other girls were freshening up for the service. A twelve-year-old girl named Marsha Stollenwerck had just left. Still in the room were Cynthia Wesley, Carole Robertson, Addie Mae, and Sarah Collins.

There was little being said. The girls were checking themselves out in the mirror, straightening dresses, running hands over their hair. Sarah had just turned on the water to wash her hands and glanced to her right, watching her sister Addie fussing with the sash of Denise's dress, which had come undone; she was retying the bow on it.

Suddenly, there was a sharp blast, and Sarah saw the outside wall crumbling. She caught just a glimpse of it— bricks and mortar and glass and wire gauge flying through the air. The exterior wall of the church was thirty inches thick, composed of stone and brick. The force of the blast blew out the section under the window and fragmented the stone and brick, as well as the limestone sills of the double window. A huge gaping hole appeared.

But Sarah didn't see that. She had already fallen blinded and bleeding and was screaming hysterically for her sister: "Addie! Addie! Addie!"

But there was no sound from Addie . . . or from Carole or Cynthia or Denise.

Upstairs, in the sanctuary, the sound of the blast brought a moment of stunned silence. Then: "We've been bombed!" someone screamed. The clock in the sanctuary stopped at 10:22.

To some it had sounded like a loud crack of thunder, almost ear-splitting. To others it seemed like a dull thud, like someone thumping a big washtub. And to some there was no sound at all, just things flying and falling wildly through the air, glass breaking, doors flipping open—a sudden wave of heat riding silently through their church.

Marsha Stollenwerck, who had been in the lounge until a few minutes before the blast, told the FBI that she had heard "a big noise" and had tried to run out the back door of the church—but she was pushed back, she had said, as if by some invisible force. Then she ran to the main entrance, located on the Sixth Avenue side, and went out.

Mrs. Young, who had moments before been talking with Denise McNair, was talking to some other children when the explosion occurred. She grabbed those nearby and fell to the floor. In the moment of panic that followed, she saw smoke billowing from the lounge area and feared the worst. She took the hands of the children near her and led them up the stairs and out the Sixth Avenue entrance. As they departed, they shot hasty glances about the church interior. Most of the large, stained-glass windows were broken;

in one, the body of Jesus on the cross remained intact, but the head had been blown away.

Mamie Grier, the teacher who had been suspicious of the green Chevy with the Confederate flag on it, was conducting an adult Sunday school class in the choir loft. Attending were Earline Tankersley, Ida Freeman, Maggie Webb, and Maxine McNair, Denise's mother, who was the last to arrive. The class was ending when the bomb went off; the sound seemed to come from the basement, on the Sixteenth Street side. Maxine McNair began to scream. She jumped up and ran out and circled behind the church, running up the alley to the Sixth Avenue side of the church, the main entrance. Mrs. Tankersley followed, later recalling that she was in such shock she couldn't remember exactly what had happened, only that they were outside, running.

In Ella Demand's classroom, from which Carole and Cynthia had been excused so they could go to the lounge, the explosion was not heard at all, said the instructor. She was suddenly aware of glass breaking and felt a surge of air move through the room. Then she saw smoke billowing in the hallways and heard screams.

In Mrs. Clevon Phillips's class, the four girls who remained there after Denise left for the ladies' lounge were unhurt. Their teacher led them up the stairs to the main sanctuary, then out the Sixth Avenue door.

In the lounge area, which had taken the brunt of the explosion, girls were screaming and crying, groping their way through the dust and smoke. The Reverend John Cross, the pastor, appeared in the hallway to help search for victims; he was bleeding from the head. As the adult church members began calling out names, it became clear that there were people who had been in the part of the building that was now reduced to rubble.

By then medical rescue units were on the scene, and police urged church members and bystanders to back away. Someone spotted a shoe, and a woman cried out that it belonged to Denise McNair. Her sobs mingled with the endless wail of ambulances.

One by one, the girls were pulled from the debris. Three were apparently dead on the spot, witnesses said. One man told the FBI later that although he heard one girl moan he felt she was near death. A fifth girl, badly injured and later identified as Sarah Collins, was alive, and an ambulance driver said he heard her mutter something. According to him, the girl said, "I saw two white men run through and then the wall fell down. I thought they were reporters. God will save me."

The weeks of threats and hoaxes had finally crashed down upon the church and its people, taking the lives of four innocent victims, girls who had not directly taken part in the civil rights marches or the attempt to desegregate the schools.

They had come to praise the Lord. Now they were dead.

3

————
————
————

In the moments following the explosion, scores of angry blacks gathered at the intersection of Sixteenth Street and Seventh Avenue North. Police, wearing helmets and holding shotguns, kept the crowd away from the church, but some young men in the crowd threw rocks and bricks. Cars driven by whites were pelted; some were overturned. Several vacant houses and a small shop were torched.

Before the day was over, racial violence had claimed the lives of two other black youths. Sixteen-year-old Johnny Robinson was shot in the back by police as he ran down an alley near the church, after a rock fight between black and white teenagers. Police said Robinson had been part of a group of teenagers that threw rocks at police.

The Reverend Cross, still bewildered by the tragedy that had struck his parishioners, told the Associated Press, "We've been expecting this all along, waiting for it, knowing it would come, wondering when." Later, he added, "I've received half a dozen bomb threats since last April. We've searched the church several times. We've called off nighttime meetings, because we felt it would be just too dangerous to gather, even if only to pray. We haven't underestimated the extremists. We've known right along there were people in this town capable of anything. Even this."

Hundreds of persons, meanwhile, had hurried to University Hospital to find out the fate of those rushed there earlier by ambulance. Guards kept the crowd back from the door. "Anguish was a living nightmare," wrote Lou Isaacson, a reporter for *The Birmingham News,* as he witnessed the fathers and mothers who came in sobbing to identify the girls, "victim by victim, scream by scream."

The only survivor in the women's lounge was Sarah Collins. She had screamed for her sister in the hellish moment after the explosion; then, blinded, lay in the rubble crying softly. "I didn't know what had happened," she said later. "I was calling for Addie because I thought she and the others had run out of there and I wanted her to come help me. I never went unconscious. I just couldn't see and I wanted to get out of there."

She had twenty-one pieces of glass in her face and eyes, and more in the chest and legs. A deep cut on her right leg would leave a scar for the rest of her life. She was taken by ambulance to University Hospital, where doctors felt she would lose sight in the right eye but could retain vision in the left. For days she would lie in the hospital room with bandages across both eyes, wondering what had happened. Family members did not immediately tell her about Addie or the three other girls who had been in the lounge with her, but Sarah would later say that she knew something bad had happened to her sister. And one day she overheard the nurses talking in hushed tones, and she knew Addie was dead.

She would remain in the hospital for two months. When she was released, she could see from the left eye but had a glass right eye.

Gertrude Wesley, Cynthia's mother, was in shock when she heard of the bombing and the death of her daughter, whom she and her husband, Claude, had adopted at the age of six. Later, she would recall:

> I remembered the Saturday night before. Cynthia was at home and she was reading the newspaper and she came across a story in the obituary column about a little baby dying. And she came to me and showed me the paper. She said, "I didn't know babies died like

15

that. I just thought old people died." And I said to her, "Well, when you go into a flower garden you don't always get something in bloom. Sometimes you pick a bud. See, the Lord wanted a bud this time, and he took that baby." And Cynthia thought about it and said, "Oh."

Next morning she was getting ready to go to church. And I told her about her slip showing and telling her to be careful about your appearance, because you never know how you're coming home. And she never did come home again. It really got to me. I kept thinking about her talking about the baby dying and me saying something about the Lord taking a bud, and about never knowing how you're coming back. She never came back. I didn't see her anymore. And I didn't want to see her that way.

Alpha Robertson, Carole's mother, was a member of the church but had not attended Sunday school. She had been at home getting ready for the main service when the telephone rang; someone called to tell her a bomb had exploded. She rushed to the church. Her husband, Alvin, who attended St. John AME Church, was already there with other relatives.

"I didn't know at the time about Carole," Mrs. Robertson would recall later. "I was there and everybody was rolling around trying to find out something, and my husband came up and told me to go home. He asked Lorenzo 'Piper' Davis, a friend of ours, to take me home. He stopped by Sardis Church for his wife and she came to my house to wait with me."

It was a short time later that another call came—this time announcing that Carole had been killed. In the shock and grief that followed, Mrs. Robertson would recall the last hours of Carole's life:

She was wearing medium high-heeled shoes, the first time she had ever worn them. We had bought them the day before. She and I had gone shopping and we

16

found the shoes, which were shiny black ones. She liked them. We went to Odom, Bowers, and White, which was a department store in the downtown. And we also picked her out a winter coat and put it on layaway. Before we left, Carole also found this necklace which she liked, so we bought it, too. And on that Sunday morning she wore the new shoes and her necklace. After the bombing, I think some weeks after, Mrs. Lillian S. Moore of the Davenport and Harris Funeral Home, came and brought me the shoes. There wasn't a scratch on them. Not one mark. I kept them for years and years, but finally I gave them to my other daughter, but she couldn't wear them because they were not the right size. But she still has them. About a week after it happened, I had a friend call the store and told them to take Carole's winter coat off layaway, that we wouldn't be getting it.

The next day, Monday, September 16, the Robertsons had the crushing duty of planning their daughter's funeral. They decided to have it quickly, at St. John, where Mr. Robertson was a member. Meanwhile, plans were being made for a mass funeral with the Reverend Martin Luther King, Jr., presiding. "We didn't know at first about that," Mrs. Robertson said, "and we had just made our own plans for Carole."

That Monday night King and several ministers came to the Robertson home to ask them to delay Carole's funeral for a day and have it included with the other three victims. Mrs. Robertson declined. Carole's funeral was held that Tuesday, September 17, at St. John AME Church, with the Reverend Cross officiating; nearly two thousand persons crammed inside the church and stood in the street outside. Gazing down on the flower-banked casket, Cross spoke somberly: "This atrocious act was committed not against race, but against all freedom-loving persons in the world. Somehow, out of this dastardly act, we have been brought together again as never before. May we not seek revenge against those who are guilty, but find our refuge in love and the words of Paul, who said, 'All things work together for good for those who love God.'"

The Reverend C. E. Thomas, pastor of St. John, told the gathering: "I want to speak to all who are here, people of both races and many creeds. I am speaking for the ministers of this city. Keep cool heads. We cannot win freedom with violence." Several hundred people were waiting outside the church as the casket was carried out and placed in a hearse to be taken to Shadow Lawn Cemetery.

On Wednesday, September 18, a crowd estimated at seven thousand gathered in and around the Sixth Avenue Baptist Church, about a mile from the bombed church. Most stood out in the streets. King led the services for Cynthia Wesley, Addie Mae Collins, and Carol Denise McNair, calling them "the modern heroines of a holy crusade." As many as two thousand may have jammed into the church itself, straining to hear King's words above the shouts of agony that punctuated the service; many in the church wept.

"We must not harbor the desire to retaliate with violence," King declared. "The deaths may well serve as the redemptive force that brings light to this dark city."

Several times during the service, members of the family or girls in the choir broke down, crying; three women collapsed and were helped from the church. Then it was over, and the pallbearers took the caskets, one by one, and edged them out into the afternoon sunlight. As they appeared at the church entrance the crowd outside reacted: some moaned and wailed; some cried out hysterically. The caskets were put in the waiting hearses then, and the journey to two cemeteries began. As the processional left the church some of the young men in the crowd began to shout insults at white spectators and police; Captain James Lay, a black civil defense official, with police officers standing behind him, quieted them down, and they finally dispersed.

The funeral entourage for Denise McNair wended its

way through the southwest section of the city and into the rolling, wooded Shadow Lawn Cemetery. Flowers were still piled freshly on Carole Robertson's grave. The procession for Cynthia Wesley and Addie Collins moved slowly to Woodlawn Cemetery in the city's east side, on a slope near the airport.

4

On the afternoon of the bombing about two thousand whites had gathered in the suburb of Midfield to hold a rally protesting the desegregation of West End High School, which had been ordered by federal court. But the planned cavalcade into Birmingham was called off because of the racially tense situation. At the rally, the Reverend Ferrell Griswold condemned the bombers and said he hoped they would be quickly apprehended. The crowd applauded him. Then, a white teenager was cheered when he strung up an effigy labeled "Kennedy."

Unaware of either the bombing or the rally, two black teenage brothers were riding double on a bike along Docena Road, about four miles from downtown Birmingham. The two-lane stretch slips by oak, pine, and mimosa trees rising from a tangle of swamp grass, poison ivy, and kudzu, the vines clinging to old fencing around industrial property. Virgil Ware, thirteen, was sitting on the handle bars; his brother, James, sixteen, was pedaling. They were returning from a junkyard, where they had hoped to get a used bike. It would be used for business, as Virgil had just landed a paper route with *The Birmingham News.*

They made the three-mile journey after attending Sunday School that morning. But the bike was not ready. Virgil was an ambitious young fellow who hoped one day to be an attorney. His favorite TV show was "Perry Mason," and family members said that he always figured out who was the guilty party.

Now it was after 4 P.M. and they were headed home, back to Pratt City, a middle-class black community outside Birmingham. As they coasted along, a red motorbike approached from the opposite direction, a Confederate flag whipping in the wind. There were two riders. As they neared each other, two quick shots rang out. Virgil fell back and then slumped sideways off the bike, falling into a roadside ditch. James quickly came to a halt and hurried to his brother's side.

"Ware, I been shot," Virgil cried. He always called his big brother by their last name.

"No, you ain't," said James in disbelief. "Just stop tremblin' and you'll be okay."

But Virgil did not speak again. Remembering that moment forty years later, James Ware bluntly intones: "That's all he said. He said, 'Ware, I been shot.' He had been hit in the left cheek and in the chest. Earlier, he had told me that we could get home quicker if we walked along the railroad tracks. But I told him I could pedal the bike real fast. I wish I had listened to him."

The red motorbike had sped on. A white couple passing by saw the black youth lying by the roadside and stopped their car to assist. The man felt Virgil's pulse and said it appeared to be stopped. He and the woman hurried to tell Virgil's family, so James could stay with his brother. The time of death has been estimated at 4:45 P.M., although the coroner's report later said the approximate time was 5:05 P.M. Virgil Ware was the last African American killed in the civil rights movement during that tumultuous year of 1963.

Interviewed in 2003, retired lawman Dan Jordan recalls getting a report late in the afternoon that a black youth had been shot and killed. In 1963 he was thirty-four, an investigator for the Jefferson County sheriff's department. A police alert had been sent on radio, a BOLO ("Be On the Lookout") for two white youths on a red motorcycle. "I remember immediately going out there to the scene," Jordan says. "It was a desolate area then, and looks about the same today."

The city had been in violent upheaval in the wake of the

bombing; the atmosphere was volatile. Jordan goes on: "We then went by the victim's residence, the Ware home in Pratt City. But there were a lot of people there because of Virgil's death, family members and friends, and we didn't want to disturb them right then."

There had not been much information on the suspects other than the sketchy details that James Ware had given. But about that time Jordan got a message from the office to call a friend of his, Paul Couch, an officer with the Mountain Brook Police Department. Jordan got to a phone. The news his friend related was stunning: "Couch was off duty that day and said he was riding in his private car when he heard the BOLO about a red motorcycle with two white riders," Jordan says. "He told me he had seen the motorbike and got the tag number. And he said he even thought he saw a pistol bulging in the back pocket of the boy riding on the rear of the motorbike. A red motorbike, he called it. So we ran the tag and got the address."

The motorcycle was registered to Michael Lee Farley, sixteen. Earlier that day, Farley and a friend, Larry Joe Sims, also sixteen, had attended the rally to oppose federal court-ordered desegregation of public schools. After several short speeches, David Orange, a captain in the Jefferson County sheriff's department, suggested that the rally and a planned motorcade be called off because of the bombing. The crowd dispersed. But Farley and Sims (both were Eagle Scouts) stopped off at the National States Rights Party office. Farley bought a Confederate flag for forty cents and placed it on the motor scooter. Meanwhile, some friends warned them of blacks throwing rocks and bricks at whites. The two got on the motorbike and headed for home. Fate brought them onto Docena Road at the same time that Virgil and James Ware were pedaling home.

Jordan and his partner, J. A. McAlpine, went the next day to the Farley home and questioned the teen. He denied any involvement. They then went to the Sims home. Larry Joe Sims, who loved playing guitar and listening to the Beach Boys, sobbed as he told of the shooting, saying the

.22 caliber pistol belonged to Farley and had been handed to him earlier. When they saw the two black youths on the bicycle, Sims said Farley shouted at him, "Scare 'em." He said he closed his eyes and fired the gun with his left hand (he was right-handed). He was afraid then that he had hit one of the youths in the leg. They then rode to a friend's house and asked him to hide the gun.

In January 1964 Sims was found guilty of manslaughter and given seven months probation; a few weeks later Farley pleaded guilty and received an identical sentence of probation. When the first sentence was announced, Lorene Ware, Virgil's mother, had broken down and wept in anguish. Sims's attorney Roderick Beddow, Sr. had gone to her and placed a hand on her shoulder. "What's the matter?" he asked. "If it had been your boy who did the shooting, I'd have done the same for him."

Sims went on to graduate from Auburn University and then went into the Army, volunteering to go to Vietnam, saying he had "a debt to pay to society." Years later, he told *Time* magazine reporter Tim Padgett that his left arm still bothered him. He said if he saw Virgil some day in Heaven he would tell him: "Your death was for something. It helped change society. It changed me."

When told that Lorene Ware had written a plea to U.S. Senator John Sparkman to keep her remaining sons out of the Army during the Vietnam War, Sims uttered in a choked voice, "Thank God." Farley, meanwhile, refused to talk about the case.

In 2004, the Reverend Griswold's son, John, forty, said his father often recounted that day in 1963: "My father was a Coushatta Indian. On that day at the rally he condemned the bombings and hoped the guilty were caught. Later, when others got up and talked about racial things, he said he was leaving because that kind of talk led to people doing nutty things. And he refused to speak at another rally that was held when the atmosphere was ugly. The shooting death of the black boy haunted him for the rest of his life. In later years he rode a motorcycle protesting nuclear power. He also became a friend with the Reverend Ralph Abernathy, who was Martin Luther King's right-hand man." He said after September 15, 1963, his father "re-focused" on desegregation issues, telling friends: "You have to change hearts before you tackle politics."

Virgil Ware's brother, Melvin, who was fourteen at the time, vividly recalls that Sunday: "I remember he asked me if I wanted to go with him and James. I said I didn't want to. We had come back from Sunday school. I didn't want them to go. I just had a feeling. . . . So I stayed at home and a football game came on the TV. And while I was watching that, they interrupted with the news that the church in Birmingham had been bombed and that four girls had been killed." He says he has forgiven those who killed his brother. "I don't hold any animosity. At one time I wanted to kill them. But I started going to church more regularly. You can't hate and be a Christian. You have to forgive to be forgiven. I still feel like it was yesterday; I still dream about it."

A sister, Joyce, who was ten in 1963, says she has not forgiven nor forgotten. "I haven't forgave him, Lord knows I haven't," she says. "If I saw them I would ask why they killed my brother."

If Virgil Ware's death was given sparse note in 1963, his final resting place was even less visible. His grave was in an abandoned cemetery overgrown with scrub pine, some hardwood, and thick underbrush. It lay at the bottom of a small slope, a muddy square kept free of wild growth by his sister, Joyce. She cleaned it every Mother's Day. "Momma told me to do it, and I do exactly that," she says. A small spray of blue carnations was the only décor. Visiting the site, she speaks aloud: "Virgil, I brought you some company." On that evening in 2003, the only light at the scene were the scores of fireflies whose faint glimmer was a reminder of that summer of lost youth in Birmingham. *Time* magazine ran a story about Virgil in 2003; the response from readers generated more than $10,000 donated to a civil rights group. Virgil was re-interred in May 2004 at the Carver Memorial Gardens, and a bronze etching of the boy's face was placed over the grave. A ceremony was held and the Ensley High Choir sang "We Shall Overcome." He was at last remembered.

On the morning of the bombing, services were about to start at the West End Methodist Church when Pastor O. S. Gamble received an anonymous telephone call: "Dr. Gamble, the Sixteenth Street Negro Church has been bombed." After confirming the news, he conducted the service. At the conclusion, he said, "I have an announcement to make. A Negro church has been bombed. The Sixteenth Street Baptist Church. I do not know if there has been loss of life." There was a stunned stillness, and then some in the congregation began to weep. "This is not right," the minister added. "All who care, come to the altar and pray." Later, he told *The Birmingham News* that more than 500 people came forward, kneeling at the altar. "I have never seen such a response in my life. It was the greatest service I have ever been in."

In the rock-throwing melee that occurred in the vicinity of the church, a white youth, Dennis Robertson, sixteen, was returning home from his job at the farmer's market. He was struck in the face and knocked unconscious. He was in a coma for several days before slowly recovering.

Not everyone in the city had been hoping for harmony in the days before the bombing. Bull Connor, in a speech before a group of whites at the Graymont Armory, was quoted in *The Birmingham News:* "One of the best things we ever did was get that bunch of dogs on the police force." He then added, "We had the reputation of being the most segregated town in America. I thought that was an honor. It's a shame now that we have to talk about hiring Negro policemen."

C. Murphy Archibald, of Union Springs, a sophomore at Birmingham-Southern College, years later would remember those times in Birmingham. "At the college, some of us were involved in the civil-rights movement. We'd go over to Miles College, which is a historically black college, to lend support. There was one student at Birmingham-Southern, Marty Turnipseed, who was quite an activist. She joined in some of the sit-ins and was kicked out of school. And I remember the president, Howard Phillips, getting the students together in Munger Hall and telling us: 'There will be no rocking of the boat.' He didn't want our students involved in the civil rights movement. I remember being there the night Joan Baez came to Miles College, and the place was packed. When she sang 'We Shall Overcome,' everyone joined in. And it was a moving moment, with her voice hanging out over the crowd." After September 15, 1963, he said, hearing the song held a deeper meaning. He was walking to church about six blocks away when the explosion occurred. "I heard it, and I knew it was something bad," he said.

The FBI sent dozens of agents into Birmingham for the most intense probe since the search for gangland figure John Dillinger in the 1930s. In the aftermath of the bombing there were shock and rage among the black leadership of Birmingham and Alabama. President Kennedy, who had ordered the Justice Department to send the FBI, expressed grief for the families of the four victims and also sent former Army football coach Earl "Red" Blaik and former secretary of the army Kenneth Royall to Birmingham to meet with both black and white leaders. Kennedy invited a group of city leaders to come to the White House and meet with him. Blacks asked the president to send federal troops into the city, but he declined.

Governor George Wallace, meanwhile, was targeted with an injunction by the state's five federal judges, led by U.S. District Judge Frank M. Johnson, Jr., to stand aside in his efforts to block school desegregation. Wallace reacted in character. He told reporters, "The federal courts—through the Kennedys—have laid the predicate that they will allow the Justice Department to jail the governor of Alabama without benefit of trial or jury, and I resent it." The bombing that took four lives, the governor said, was a "dastardly act by a demented fool . . . who has universal hate in his heart."

On Monday at the weekly noon meeting of the Young Men's Business Club, attorney Charles Morgan, Jr., obtained permission to read a statement. He began by asking, "Who did it?" and proceeded to lay the blame for the bombing on all Alabama residents who had remained silent on the issue of desegregation or who had vowed to maintain the racial status quo. "We are a mass of intolerance and bigotry and stand indicted before our young," he read. "We are cursed by the failure of each of us to accept responsibility, by our defense of an already dead institution." He concluded, "Every person in this community who has in any way contributed to the popularity of hatred is at least as guilty, or more so, as the demented fool who threw that bomb."

The reaction of the state press was mixed. "May God Forgive Us," lamented an editorial in the Talladega *Daily Home*: "This should be Alabama's universal cry in the wake of our blackest day. May God forgive this newspaper and all others for any mishandling of news, any editorial comments which may have helped to sow the seeds of violence. May God forgive the bombers who put a bloody 'amen' to the hour of worship." Later, it added, "The shame will be ours forever."

In its September 16 edition, *The Birmingham News*'s editorial, entitled "The Shock and Shame," read: "Not one word or a million makes up for the deaths of four innocent children in the Sunday School bombing yesterday morning." It added, "It is yet possible, despite the host of unsolved bombings, that what must be a small band of men will be arrested and tried for what must be called outright murder wholly premeditated and carried out. Every white man certainly should be asking himself how he would feel if for years the unidentified had made his wife, his children, his home, his church, the object of such hatred." It concluded, "May God grant us a strength of leadership and a wisdom we have yet to attain. Beyond this prayer nothing now makes much sense."

The *Cullman Times* blamed national leaders for the bombing. "Blood is on the hands of those persons who have promoted racism for their own selfish interests. There is no doubt the Kennedys and Martin Luther King and numerous others have promoted the issues for their own personal gain."

The *Valley Voice,* a northwest Alabama weekly, said that "Birmingham, shocked and shamed and knocked to its knees by 10 sticks of dynamite, is to be pitied. What more, we may ask, can happen?"

The *Selma Times-Journal* pondered, "It is difficult for decent, civilized people to express what is in their hearts."

The *Birmingham News* carried a letter from a "G. Jones" of Huntsville, who wrote to the editor: "I wonder if the Negroes of Birmingham have stopped long enough to try to figure out who is at the root of all their troubles. Two men—John and Bobby Kennedy. If the thought has not occurred to them, they should think it over."

The week of the bombing, U.S. District Judge Clarence Allgood convened a federal grand jury to deal with what he said was a band of citizens who were making a mockery of federal law. He had originally notified the jurors to be there because of the wave of violence that was sweeping Birmingham in reaction to federal court orders regarding school desegregation. "In recent weeks we have witnessed what amounts to mockery of our laws, a mockery by those who would cut the very roots of our American system of justice," he said, "who in doing so would starve the growth of our way of life and snuff out human life with insane fury and irrationality. Sunday's bombing of a Negro church—a place of worship—where the lives of four children were taken, is a hideous example. I can think of no greater heresy or a more blackening sin against humanity."

5

————
————
————

Birmingham's mayor, Albert Boutwell, a former lieutenant governor of Alabama, had wept when he learned of
the bombing. He called the city council into emergency
session and issued a resolution condemning the bombing
and expressing sympathy for the bereaved families. The
resolution read: "The horrified indignation of our community at this barbaric and senseless atrocity can best be expressed by the unanimous and continued determination of
every citizen not only to bring these criminals to justice,
but to make certain that no such crime is ever again perpetrated here."

The next day, each of the families was sent a telegram
from Boutwell and the council: "Writing as we do in pro-
found sorrow and Christian sincerity, we the Mayor and
the City Council convey to you and all your loved ones the
grief we share with you. Each of us prays the almighty God
that he, in his infinite compassion and tender mercy, will
comfort your hearts and strengthen your faith. We say this
and pray in the name of the whole city and its people."

Boutwell was not outspoken on the issue of segregation,
but he did say what was expected of a southern politician
in those days. Shortly after his election he remarked, "I am
determined that we are going to defend, I hope maintain,
segregation, but we are not going to be a city of unre-
strained and unhampered mockery of the law."

Reaction across the nation to the bombing was swift: The

County of Los Angeles fired off a telegram to Boutwell, notifying him that the regular meeting of the board of supervisors had been canceled in memory of the four girls, and scrolls were sent to their families. The city council of Ann Arbor, Michigan, sent a thousand-dollar money order to Alabama Governor Wallace to be used in a reward fund being established. Wallace forwarded the money to the Birmingham city council.

Actually, Boutwell and the council had begun a reward fund several weeks earlier, hoping that a large windfall would inspire witnesses to come forward with information on other bombings. The fund had been announced August 21, the day after the bombing of the home of Arthur Shores, in a statement proclaiming that

> The four bombing atrocities in Birmingham since April 2nd are intolerable. All bombings are. We have been charged with responsibility to stand behind law enforcement agencies of this city in protecting the safety of its citizens. Two homes, a department store, and a motel have thus far been struck. The best possible protection for the future safety . . . is the immediate jailing and punishment of every individual who has any hand in the despicable and cowardly outrages against human life and public order.
>
> The early arrest of the criminal hoodlums and their conviction, with maximum penalties, is the surest way to put an end to these atrocities. The safety of schools, churches, and homes demands it. The most important contribution any citizen can make is useful information, clues or leads; and the second most important is a contribution, regardless of amount, to this reward fund.

Later he added, "We will not tolerate bombings, and we will not tolerate mobs or crowds that can explode into violence, no matter who they are."

City officials hoped for at least $50,000, but pledges came in slowly. Then, after the bombing of the church, there was a sudden surge of pledges and checks, mostly from whites in Birmingham and other Alabama towns. The Good Citizens Club of Sylacauga sent $25. The Shades Valley Council of Garden Clubs donated $10. Some individuals sent as little as a dollar or two. Others, such as Mervyn H. Sterne, pledged $1,000; the Pratt Coal Company pledged $500; the Downtown Action Committee, $2,000; and *The Birmingham News* and *Birmingham Post-Herald,* $4,000.

But others were not so sympathetic. An envelope arrived at the Birmingham City Hall addressed to the reward fund. It was stuffed full of money—$500 in Confederate bills, and $100,000 in play money. The letter had a return address for "A. J. Ramage, 104 Leopold St., Bay St. Louis, Miss." Another letter, which contained one stamp, read, "I would like to contribute one cancelled 5 cent postage stamp to the Martin Luther King Son of Hell fund." It was signed, "H. H. Carpenter, 7704 6th Ave., North."

On September 18, just three days after the church bombing, the reward fund had topped $76,000. Dr. John H. Buchanan, chaplain of the Birmingham Baptist Hospitals and a member of the reward fund board of trustees, wrote to Boutwell declaring, "May I assure you, as I have contacted the donors of this fund, that the overwhelming majority of our Birmingham citizens, both white and colored, are aroused that our fair city shall no longer be made a victim of a lawless group which endangers life and property in Birmingham."

But September passed into November, and then the winter. Then 1964 came and went, and still no information had come forth that would lead to an arrest and prosecution. The stipulations of the fund said the information must be received before December 31, 1964. It never came.

In the days following the bombing, FBI agents pursued hundreds of leads and dogged the trail of known Ku Klux Klan members, bringing them in for questioning and polygraph testing. At that point, the roles of the state of Alabama and the Birmingham Police Department were minimal. But on September 30, 1963, Colonel Al Lingo, director of the Alabama Department of Public Safety, held a press conference to make the stunning announcement that three Birmingham men had been arrested. However, the three—Robert Edward Chambliss, John Wesley Hall, and Charles Cagle—were charged not with murder or as participants in a conspiracy to bomb the church, but rather with possession of dynamite, a misdemeanor. They were fined $1,000 and given six-month sentences, which were later suspended.

In January of 1965, attorney James O. Haley, who was overseer of the reward fund, wrote Boutwell that no information had been furnished by the deadline: "It seems we are now under obligation to refund the money that has been paid and to release the pledgers from their commitment unless information has been furnished which is reasonably calculated to lead to the arrest and conviction of one or more parties in connection with the several bombings." On March 18, 1965, the trustees of the reward fund voted to refund the money, which in cash and pledges had reached $79,764. Some of the cash donors could not be contacted, and $113 left over was given to the Red Cross. Another contribution of $6 was given to Haley's firm to help cover the cost of postage for mailing cash back to donors.

While the FBI persisted in its probe over the coming months, there was only one federal arrest made—that occurring after a klansman swung at agents questioning him. The FBI had pursued the case under Reconstruction-era civil rights legislation intended to combat KKK terror. But the statute of limitations for the federal offense expired in five years. Thus, on September 15, 1968, as no arrests had been made, the FBI's official involvement ended. It seemed the bombing would simply fade into history, unsolved.

IN MEMORY OF

DENISE MCNAIR CYNTHIA WESLEY ADDIE MAE COLLINS CAROL ROBERTSON

THEIR LIVES WERE TAKEN BY UNKNOWN PARTIES ON SEPTEMBER 15, 1963 WHEN THE SIXTEENTH STREET BAPTIST CHURCH WAS BOMBED.

"MAY MEN LEARN TO REPLACE BITTERNESS AND VIOLENCE WITH LOVE AND UNDERSTANDING"

A plaque in the church sanctuary memorializes the girls who died in the explosion. (Photo by Frank Sikora)

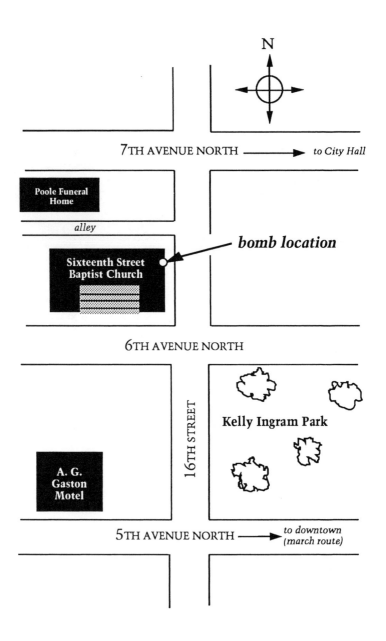

N

7TH AVENUE NORTH ➝ *to City Hall*

Poole Funeral
Home

alley

Sixteenth Street
Baptist Church

bomb location

6TH AVENUE NORTH

Kelly Ingram Park

16TH STREET

A. G.
Gaston
Motel

5TH AVENUE NORTH ➝ *to downtown
(march route)*

Birmingham's Sixteenth Street Baptist Church has served as a focus of black community life since its founding in 1873, just two years after the city was incorporated. The surrounding neighborhood, known as the near west side, is located a few blocks from the skyscrapers and public buildings of downtown Birmingham. In 1963, civil rights activists held rallies and meetings at the church, and demonstrators gathered across the street in Kelly Ingram Park to organize marches down Fifth Avenue to City Hall. The black-owned A. G. Gaston Motel was among several buildings bombed during the spring of 1963, and on September 15, a large bomb exploded at the church, killing four girls. The bomb had been hidden underneath an exterior staircase near the rear of the building, along the Sixteenth Street side; the staircase was blown away by the explosion and was not replaced. In the years since, downtown expansion and urban renewal have claimed much of the neighborhood, and in 1988 the city announced plans for a civil rights museum on the land directly across Sixth Avenue from the front entrance of the church. (Photo and map by Paula Dennis)

Rescue workers remove one of the victims of the blast, which killed four and injured twenty. (Courtesy *The Birmingham News*)

Fire and police officials examine what was left of the women's lounge in the church basement, which took the main impact of the explosion. The crater in the ground shows where the bomb was placed, just outside the two-foot-thick stone and masonry wall. (Courtesy *The Birmingham News*)

A Birmingham police officer, armed with a shotgun, stands guard outside the church. Rioting broke out following the explosion, and one teenager was fatally shot by police. (Courtesy *The Birmingham News*)

Some mourners collapsed during funerals for the bombing victims. (Courtesy
The Birmingham News)

In the wake of the bombing, much of the world viewed images of the destruction on television and in newspapers. One widely published news photo showed a stained-glass window from the sanctuary, in which it appeared that the head of Christ had been blasted off his body. A year later, a large new window showing a black Jesus on the cross was presented to the Sixteenth Street Baptist Church as a memorial gift from the people of Wales. It is mounted above the main entrance to the church. (Photo by Paula Dennis)

BY PERSON OR PERSONS
UNKNOWN

6

There is no statute of limitations on murder. And in 1970, seven years after the bombing, a twenty-eight-year-old lawyer named William J. Baxley, who was newly elected attorney general of Alabama, made it clear to his staff that the bombing of the church was an active case that would be pursued.

Baxley was of medium height and build, with dark brown hair that was, in 1970, worn long enough to ramble over the edge of his shirt collar. His brown eyes were framed by features that were disarmingly boyish. He had a temper, and a deep, loud voice that became deeper and louder when his patience was tried. Baxley hailed from an aristocratic south Alabama family, and he had ambitions to be governor. One of his earliest memories had been of a game in which he pretended to be elected to the state's highest office.

When the church had been bombed, Baxley was in his final year of law school at The University of Alabama. Earlier that year, he had watched with other white students as Governor Wallace had attempted to keep two blacks, Vivian Malone and James Hood, from being admitted to the university. When he heard about the girls killed at the church, "it just made me sick," he said later. "I wanted to do something. I told a friend of mine that one day I was going to do something about it. I was in a fraternity, and most of the guys were thinking about football and their studies.

But I was sick. I wondered who could do something like that, kill four kids."

When he graduated in 1964, he worked for a year as a law clerk for the Alabama Supreme Court, then returned home to Dothan, a small city in the southeastern corner of the state. A vacancy occurred in the office of district attorney, and Baxley was appointed to it. He had actively sought the post, which he viewed as a stepping stone to one day becoming Alabama's attorney general.

In 1970 he did seek that office and won, defeating the incumbent, MacDonald Gallion. When he took office, the only thing he carried that showed he was the attorney general of Alabama was a small card issued by the state with phone numbers and instructions concerning use of the state WATS line. One day he was making a call from a phone booth, and as he looked at the card he wrote the names of the four girls, one in each corner of the card. From then on, each time he used the card to make a phone call, he would see their names.

Baxley hired dozens of attorneys, and was the first Alabama attorney general to hire a black attorney and a black woman attorney. His office pursued corrupt elected officials, cracked down on small-town speed traps, probed union violence in the state's coal industry, and blocked oil companies from drilling in Mobile Bay. There were soon hundreds of cases that his office was involved in, but over them all was the church bombing case. Friends would say the deaths of the four girls had become the controlling force in Baxley's life.

In February 1971, shortly after being sworn into office, he formed a team of attorneys and investigators to work on the bombing of the church. His first team member was Jack Shows, a husky, dark-haired man who was a former Montgomery police detective. He later brought in attorneys George Beck, George Royer, and John Yung. The attorneys were young, eager, and idealistic.

When the team was formed, Baxley called Shows to his office and showed him a book of matches. On the inside of the cover were the names of the four girls killed in the bombing.

"Here," he said, handing the matches to Shows. "See those names? This case is going to be the number one priority in my four years." As it turned out, Baxley would win reelection, and the case would be the top priority during the eight years he served as Alabama attorney general.

In many ways, Baxley was a maverick in Alabama politics; at a time when other white politicians were assailing the federal government for interfering with states rights and forcing schools to desegregate, he supported voting rights for blacks and access to public accommodations. He admired U.S. District Judge Frank M. Johnson, Jr., of Montgomery, who had handed down so many civil rights decisions. In his office Baxley had a picture of the judge and had bronze busts of Abraham Lincoln, John F. Kennedy, and Franklin D. Roosevelt. He also had a picture of Lyndon Baines Johnson. While he was liberal in his political thinking, Baxley was nonetheless respected by most law enforcement officers in Alabama. And he was a close friend of Alabama football coach Paul W. "Bear" Bryant, who often called the young attorney general; from time to time they would get together for dinner and a drink.

One Monday night during football season Baxley and Bryant met in Birmingham for dinner—"supper," Bear preferred to call it—and afterwards sat in the restaurant drinking. They seldom talked about racial matters, and the topic of the church bombing had not come up. But Baxley raised an issue that had been nagging at him since he'd attended a game in Tuscaloosa two days earlier.

"Bear," he said, "I was looking at the program during the game Saturday and I noticed that a lot of the alumni chapters sponsors ads saying how proud they are of a player who comes from their town or county in the state."

Bear nodded. "That's right. They do that."

"They run the kid's picture and where he's from and say how proud they are of him," Baxley went on.

"That's right."

"Well, I noticed that there are no black players being named in there."

Bear was silent.

"Probably makes them feel left out, I would imagine," the attorney general continued.

But the coach sipped his drink and stared ahead, saying nothing further.

Next morning, when Baxley arrived at his office in Montgomery, his secretary had a message for him: "Call Coach Bryant." He dialed the number and Bryant answered.

"You remember what we talked about last night?" Bear asked.

"We talked about a lot of things," said Baxley.

"No, you were talking about the ads in the football programs and the black players."

"I remember."

"Well, Bill, I don't want to get involved directly in this," Bear said. "But why don't you make some calls and talk to some of these local alumni groups and get them to start sponsoring ads for the black kids, too."

"Okay."

Within a few Saturdays the football programs began running the pictures of black players such as Lou Ikner and Calvin Culliver.

Early in the investigation, Baxley went to see Governor Wallace to ask that the state offer a reward in the case. The governor agreed to authorize a $10,000 reward and told Baxley, "I've always wanted them caught. You know, I said back then that they should kick out the bottom of the electric chair in this case."

Baxley had mixed feelings about the indirect role Wallace might have played in the bombings or other acts of racial violence that occurred in the 1960s. "There are two schools of thought," he told a reporter. "One says that Wallace, by his speeches and actions, caused more violence. The second says that by standing up at the schoolhouse door and all he might have prevented it. He had told people to stay away, that he would fight the battle."

By Person or Persons Unknown

Baxley's forebears in the 1800s had settled the south-eastern section of Alabama known as the Wiregrass, flat coastal-plain land that was studded with pine trees and coarse grasses that gave the area its name. His great grand-fathers had fought for the South, and one of them had been captured by the Union army. His grandfather, William Joseph Baxley, served as mayor of Dothan, the largest town in that area of the state. His father, Keener Baxley, was a cir-cuit judge. While the family was decidedly southern, and family members had pointed feelings about the Republi-can party, the party of Abraham Lincoln, they did not have the strong anti-black emotions that prevailed in other areas of Alabama.

"Dothan wasn't even founded until after the Civil War," Baxley said, speaking of his heritage. "Dothan and that part of the state was never part of the plantation belt. There just weren't a lot of slaves down there, and when the war ended not many blacks moved there. Many of them went North."

Feelings in the family were more political than racial, he said. When Herbert Hoover ran for president in 1928 as the Republican nominee, most white Alabamians sup-ported him over the Democratic nominee, Al Smith, who was Catholic. But not William Joseph Baxley, the mayor of Dothan. He voted for Smith. "My granddaddy didn't care about him being a Catholic as much as he did about Hoover being a Republican," Baxley said. "Hoover was a Republi-can, the same as Abraham Lincoln, and that was the party that he felt was responsible for the Civil War. See, grand-daddy recalled his father coming home from the war on crutches."

Baxley hired the first black assistant attorney general in state history, Myron Thompson, a native Alabamian who had earned his law degree from Yale. On the day Thomp-son was hired, Baxley called the staff into his office and announced that a black attorney was joining the team. He said he would be hiring other qualified blacks in the days to come. "Now, if any of you have a problem with that," he said, "you'd better find another job."

He also hired women attorneys, and not long after Thompson had been hired Baxley recruited the first black woman ever to be an assistant Alabama attorney general, Vanzetta Penn, a Montgomery native. Penn would later go into private practice; Thompson would go on to become the second black federal judge in Alabama.

In early 1972 the bombing investigation took a setback when John Yung told Baxley he was resigning to join the Peace Corps. Yung, a graduate of George Washington University Law School, was an aloof, aristocratic man who wore his dark hair trimmed in conservative style; his rimless glasses added to the reserved air. Friends said he was a man who rarely showed emotion. But when the staff learned he was leaving, plans were made to have a farewell party at a rustic retreat at Lake Martin, about fifty miles from Montgomery. Just about everyone on the staff showed up—except Yung. (In later years he would somewhat drily admit, "I didn't know about it.")

He left for the island of Yap in the South Pacific and was a legal counsel helping establish a government. Then, in 1974, he returned to Alabama and asked Baxley for his old job back. He was promptly rehired and once again placed on the bombing team.

7

————
————
————

Baxley's first suspect was J. B. Stoner, an attorney from Marietta, Georgia, and head of the National States Rights Party. Stoner believed that blacks should be sent to Africa, and that Hitler had been too soft on Jews. Birmingham police had often seen him in the city during the late 1950s and early 1960s. Police Chief Jamie Moore had noted that during the early morning hours of June 29, 1958, he had received a call from the Reverend Fred Shuttlesworth who said that his church, Bethel Baptist, had been bombed. The time was 1:31 A.M. At 1:48 A.M., Moore received another call, this one from a man who identified himself as "General Forrest of the Confederate Underground." The man told Moore, "We have just bombed the center of Communist integration in the South." Moore's detectives checked with Georgia authorities, who had routinely kept Stoner under watch. They reported that Stoner had left home during the night of June 27, but no one knew where he had gone.

Baxley's team tracked down an elderly ex-klansman in Georgia who knew Stoner. He agreed to meet with Alabama investigators, and indicated he might have information about Stoner that could be incriminating. Week after week, month after month, Baxley and some of his team members would visit the man, hoping he would say something to help establish a case against Stoner. But after almost two years of riding to Georgia, the team had heard nothing notable. Irritated, Baxley one day snapped, "He's scared of Stoner. He hasn't told us a thing. I'll bet we've been over there fifty times." Baxley grudgingly concluded that Stoner probably did not do the bombing of the Sixteenth Street Baptist Church.

Baxley and his team found little help from the files of local police. "They had a slim folder on the case," he would recall years later. "At the time the thinking of many whites was that blacks themselves had done the bombing to get sympathy and support from people up North. And that was the basis for the police investigation." One popular story said that some black men placed the dynamite in the alley near the church. Late that Saturday night an alcoholic black man came along, stumbled onto the box, and placed it near the rear door of the church. One local officer said Birmingham police could never locate the man. Baxley had heard such accounts before, and from the first felt that they were absurd. "It's ridiculous to think blacks would bomb their own church and kill these innocent children."

During the search for the guilty parties in the church bombing, Baxley's effort uncovered another racial murder that had occurred in January 1957. A black man named Willie Edwards, twenty-five, was a truck driver for the Sunday Dinner company in Montgomery. One day another driver was unable to come to work, and Edwards was given his route. That night as he drove along U.S. 231 just north of the city, several cars forced him off the road. Armed men told him to stand on the railing of the bridge over the rain-swollen Alabama River. Then he was ordered to jump— or he would be shot. He jumped. His body was not found until March, lodged against some debris in Lowndes Country. Baxley's team found a former KKK member who told the gruesome details, saying that a black truck driver had made socially unacceptable comments to a white woman. The KKK members mistakenly thought Edwards was the man. Efforts to bring the men to trial were blocked when a state judge, Frank Embry, said a cause of death had not been established, using the absurd argument that jumping off a bridge in itself does not cause death.

By early 1973 it was painfully clear that if Baxley were to have even the slimmest chance of breaking the case he would have to have the FBI files. He had been trying for years to obtain them, visiting FBI offices in Birmingham and Washington, always hitting a stone wall. Once, after coming back from Washington, he fumed to his staff: "The FBI tells me it's too busy to be looking up old files. I've been up there about fifteen times and can't even see J. Edgar Hoover."

Hoover's death on May 2, 1972, did not ease the FBI's rigid policy that its files were not to be shared. When Clarence Kelley was named director of the agency, Baxley made more trips to Washington. But he still couldn't get in to the director's office. To Kelley's underlings he pleaded that it was urgent that he have access to the documents, but his pleas were futile.

In 1975 Baxley tried again, once more catching a plane to the nation's capital. And, once again, he was rejected in the front offices of the FBI. Glumly, he called an old friend to have lunch before he returned to Montgomery. The friend was Jack Nelson, Washington bureau chief of the *Los Angeles Times*. Nelson, a native of Talladega, Alabama, had obtained some FBI files on the bombing under the then-new Freedom of Information Act, and had written several stories based on the files. When he received the call from Baxley that day he agreed to meet with the Alabama Attorney General.

"Where are you having lunch?" he asked.

"At the Sans Souci," Baxley replied.

But Nelson declined, saying he preferred not to dine there. The restaurant was a "fishbowl" in Washington, a place where people in high places gathered, a place where those dining often made the newspaper gossip columns. Art Buchwald had a reserved table. Nelson just didn't like going there.

"Aw, come on," Baxley insisted. "I've already got reservations."

Nelson reluctantly agreed, and they met. As they were eating Baxley mentioned the bombing case and his problems with the FBI. Then he got out his wallet, pulled out a piece of crumpled paper, and handed it across the table to Nelson. The reporter studied it and noted the names of the four girls written on it.

Baxley leaned forward over the table and declared, "I'm going to get the bastards who killed those kids."

Nelson nodded. He told Baxley that he'd do what he could to help.

Baxley had no idea how much Nelson would help. Nelson went to U.S. Attorney General Edward M. Levi and told him he had learned that the Justice Department and the FBI were hindering Alabama's efforts to investigate the church bombing by withholding information. Nelson indicated he was going to write a story. He also said that Baxley was going to bring family members of the four victims to Washington and hold a press conference on the steps of the Lincoln Memorial or the Justice Department. Several days later Nelson received a call from a Justice Department spokesman: "Hold up on the story. The FBI's going to turn over many of its files to Alabama." It was a dramatic breakthrough. Baxley later termed Nelson "one of the unsung heroes of the case."

The FBI delivered the files to Montgomery, and secretary Pauline Jackson watched as staffers lugged a box of files to Baxley's office near the state capitol. Baxley, Shows, Beck, and Yung began poring over them. It would take months to read them all and try to digest the material. While many of the Ku Klux Klan interviews were intact, there were some names blanked out; Baxley's team might read a statement but not know who made it to FBI agents in 1963 and 1964.

In the fall of 1975 Baxley's team began interviewing klansmen and former klansmen in Birmingham, arriving at front doors with grand jury subpoenas. Sometimes investigators would put the klansmen in a car and take them to Montgomery for questioning and polygraph tests.

One klansman was hauled to Montgomery in the middle of the night by Baxley's investigators. The man, an alcoholic, was shaking so badly he could barely speak. Baxley called his men aside and whispered, "I think this guy will talk if we can loosen him up." He reached into his pocket, fetched out three dollars, and told an investigator, "Here. Go get him something to drink."

The klansman drank the three-dollars' worth of cheap wine but said nothing. Baxley ordered agents to take him back to Birmingham. "I'd have been better off saving my money," he conceded.

As his investigators pursued leads obtained in the FBI files, white supremacists claimed violations of their constitutional rights. Chiropractor E. R. Fields, one of the leaders of Stoner's National States Rights Party, printed an article in the organization's newsletter, *Thunderbolt,* that charged Baxley with harassing and intimidating "white patriots." Fields, a Marietta, Georgia, resident who had formerly lived in Bessemer, also claimed that the investigation was Baxley's way of obtaining political support from "the large negro bloc vote in Alabama." He said he sent Baxley a letter "politely protesting his harassment of White people in Birmingham."

Baxley used official State of Alabama stationery for his reply:

> Dear "Dr." Fields:
> My response to your letter of February 19, 1976 is—
> kiss my ass.
> Sincerely,
> Bill Baxley
> Attorney General

Fields fired off a response in the next edition of *Thunderbolt:* "That an individual of such vile character could become Attorney General and be a serious contender for the governorship is a reflection of our times." He further charged that the bombing probe was "the continuing radical campaign of Bill Baxley to force his own personal brand of RECONSTRUCTIONIST RULE over White Alabama." White patriots, said Fields, "will see to it that he will never be elected to public office—EVER AGAIN!"

As the probe sputtered along, Baxley would sometimes speak of his frustrations to his secretary and confidential assistant, Lucy Richards, who also was from Dothan. A number of times he asked her how she felt about his pursuing a case that the FBI had not been able to break. "You're like the average Alabama person," he would say. "What do you think of this?"

And she would reply, "I think you're doing what is right, what you believe is right, and what a lot of the people in this state think is right." He would stare at her and nod in agreement. Yet, at the same time, he knew that the investigation of the church bombing could damage his chances of one day becoming governor of Alabama.

Lucy Richards, who was divorced, had been Baxley's secretary when he was district attorney in Dothan and had come to Montgomery to continue working for him. The professional relationship had flowered into romance, and on July 11, 1976, they were married in a quiet ceremony at Whitfield Memorial United Methodist Church. Baxley, one of the state's most eligible bachelors, had not told his family until ten days before the ceremony.

8

————
————
————

In late 1976 Baxley added a new investigator to his staff, forty-three-year-old Bob Eddy, from Huntsville, the city in the northern section of the state that was one of the centers of America's space industry. Eddy was a combat veteran of the Korean War, but his career in law enforcement was by no means a long one; in fact, when the bombing of the church had taken place in 1963, he had been operating a restaurant in Huntsville. He had become involved in law enforcement after a fire destroyed the restaurant; with a wife and two daughters to support, he needed a job. As luck would have it, the sheriff of Madison County needed another deputy at the time.

In 1972, Eddy helped convict a Madison County judge of soliciting sexual favors from attractive women charged with minor offenses such as speeding or writing an occasional bad check. It was a case that Baxley had prosecuted himself; he was impressed with Eddy's work and later offered him a job.

Eddy never understood the racial hatred that was so much a part of Alabama in the 1960s. He had been born and raised in Walker County, hilly mining country northwest of Birmingham. There were few blacks living in the county, and he didn't remember seeing much of them as he was growing up. But he did remember that in the late 1930s, when he was about eight, he would sometimes go with an uncle to visit relatives in adjoining Cullman

County. They would cross the Black Warrior River on a ferry, and as they approached the other side there was a large sign that read, "Nigger, don't let the sundown catch you in Cullman County."

For the first few months Eddy worked on routine cases around the state, getting home on weekends to see his wife, Peggy, and the girls. Most of the time he was living out of a motel. Then, in late January of 1977, when he was at the Coosa County Courthouse in Rockford, a town about sixty miles northeast of Montgomery, he received a call from his supervisor. "Are you at a point where you can break away?" he was asked.

"Well, not really," Eddy said. "What's up?"

"Wrap it up and come on back. Baxley wants to see you. He wants to get you started on something right away."

Curious, Eddy hurried back to Montgomery and went immediately to see his supervisor, who told him he would be working on the bombing case in Birmingham. "The church," he said. "You'll have to talk to Bill about it. But as of right now you're off of everything else except that one case."

Eddy went in to see Baxley then, and even before he could sit down the attorney general said, "You know what I want you to do?"

Eddy eased into the chair. "Yes, sir."

Baxley stood up and leaned on his desk. "I want you to go to Birmingham. I want you to go there and read everything you can on the case. I want you to talk to everyone you can—FBI, police, klansmen, people at the church. I want you to go there and stay for ninety days. I want you to send me reports when you can. If we need to see you we'll come up there. I want to know after you're there for three months if there's a chance we can make a case against anybody."

In early February Eddy went to Birmingham, a hundred miles north of Montgomery. He checked into the Holiday Inn near the downtown Civic Center. It was after 5 P.M. when he arrived, and by the time he had unloaded his gear it was night. He went to the restaurant and had a light supper, then sat drinking coffee. He liked working alone on cases, but the enormity of this investigation began to concern him. Here was a case that he knew little or nothing about, a case that was nearly fourteen years old, and he didn't know where to begin. He felt overwhelmed. After fourteen years, trails grew cold. The FBI had had dozens of crack agents working the case when it was still fresh but had never made an arrest. If they couldn't do it, how could he?

That night Eddy called FBI agent Ed Kennedy and invited him to have breakfast. Kennedy had been assigned to the FBI's Huntsville office when Eddy was with the sheriff's department there, and they had worked on some cases together. Kennedy met him next morning and they talked about the church bombing. The agent said he knew little about it. As they finished the meal, Eddy asked if Kennedy could arrange a meeting with the agent in charge, Roy Kirkpatrick. Kennedy said he would ask. Within an hour, Eddy got a telephone call from Kennedy, who said Kirkpatrick would see him that day.

The FBI office in Birmingham is on Eighth Avenue North, two blocks from the Holiday Inn, and Eddy walked there in five minutes. Kirkpatrick, an affable man in his early fifties, asked how he could help. Eddy told him that he'd like to see more files from the bombing case. Kirkpatrick said he would review the files and let Eddy read those that he was authorized to release, but others were confidential, he said, and could not be made available.

That afternoon Eddy went to the Birmingham Police Department and met Captain Jack LeGrand and Sergeant Earnest Cantrell. Both men had been with the department when the bombing occurred and had now been assigned by Mayor David Vann to work with Baxley's team while in the city. Vann once told a reporter that the Sixteenth Street Baptist Church was sacred ground. "There is no more hallowed ground in this country. It's like Gettysburg or Concord."

In 1963 Vann had been an attorney in private practice

who was placed on loan to the city to help ease the effort to desegregate. After the springtime of unrest, he had felt progress was being made—until the church was bombed. Now, as mayor, he hoped his officers could help Baxley break the case.

Captain LeGrand felt certain that a man by the name of Gary Thomas Rowe, Jr., who had been a paid FBI informer in the 1960s, had actually taken part in the bombing. Sergeant Cantrell was less certain but had strong suspicions. Cantrell was especially sensitive about the case because he had been on duty near the church on the night the bomb was set under the side steps. He told Eddy that on that night of September 14 and 15, 1963, he had been in a marked police car patrolling near the church. Sometime around 1:30 A.M. on the morning of the bombing, he and other officers were alerted to respond to a bomb threat at the Holiday Inn on Third Avenue North, about three blocks south of the church. As best Eddy could reconstruct it, the threat had been a klan diversion tactic; when officers went to the Holiday Inn, the klan bomb unit moved in and placed the dynamite at the church. The klan had also held a motorcade through the downtown that night—another apparent diversion.

A few days after arriving in Birmingham, Eddy received a telephone call from the FBI's Kirkpatrick, who said Eddy could begin reading some of the files: field reports from the scene, mostly interviews with church members. These files were more complete and detailed than the ones Baxley had obtained in Washington. Names of witnesses had been blacked out in what Baxley had seen, but in the reports Eddy saw now, names were not concealed.

Eddy began spending most days at the FBI office. Special-Agent-in-Charge Kirkpatrick provided him with an office to use and also assigned an agent to assist him. The agent was Cole Geary, a big New Englander with iron-gray hair and a tough disposition. Geary gave new meaning to the word "blunt."

The first day he saw Eddy he announced, "I hear you're working on the church bombing."

Eddy looked up at him and nodded.

Geary regarded him coolly. "I don't think much of your investigation—I think it's all politics by Bill Baxley," he said. "He doesn't have a chance. We worked that thing and couldn't do anything with it, and you're not going to, either."

His words did little to help Eddy's confidence; he was already having doubts about the project. But he stared back at Geary and managed a grin. "I hope you're wrong."

Geary shrugged. "Well, maybe I'll be wrong."

In the end, Geary would prove to be a vital figure in the case. He was supposed to supply Eddy with files that he asked for specifically. Since there was so much that Eddy didn't know about the case, it was difficult for him to know which files he should request. After several weeks, Geary began suggesting which files Eddy should ask for.

9

————
————
————

Studying the files, which contained hundreds of interviews in connection with the bombing, Eddy came across two persons who witnessed an unusual event at the church two weeks before the bombing.

One was James Edward Lay, the black civil defense captain, who told agents he saw a black, two-door 1957 Ford (fitting the description of the car Stoner and Fields were often seen in) parked near the church at about 12:10 A.M. September 2, 1963. Lay said the car was parked under a mimosa tree that grew directly in front of the concrete steps, the point where the bomb was later set and exploded. He said he saw a white man carrying a small bag walk from the Ford car to the steps. When Lay called to him, the man stopped and quickly returned to the car, which then pulled out and left. Lay said he did not clearly see the license number. Later, viewing photos of known klansmen, he picked out a picture of Tommy Blanton, Jr., as resembling the man who walked to the steps. He identified a picture of Robert Chambliss as resembling the driver.

Lay wasn't alone on the street that night. A black disc jockey, "Tall Paul" White, was also out on the sidewalk and saw the car with two men in it. Eddy needed to talk to both men, if he could find them. It was interesting to note the date of the sightings—September 2—which was to be the first day of school desegregation in Birmingham. The klansmen apparently had wanted to get their message across early, but Lay must have scared them. Later that day there was disorder at West End High School when several black students attempted to be admitted. Hundreds of white students jeered and shouted insults at the black students. Klan members had signs on their cars that read, "Keep West End White."

Eddy tracked down Civil Defense Captain Lay, a husky man who was cooperative but not especially friendly. He agreed to talk but made it clear he could not be counted on to testify. "I don't want to get involved with this," he said. "I tried to tell them about this back when it happened, but nobody listened to me. So I don't want 'em coming to me now for help. I won't testify in court."

Eddy wasn't sure why Lay had such strong feelings, but he refused to budge. Even when told there was a chance to get the persons responsible for murdering the four girls, he simply shook his head.

The disc jockey Tall Paul White was twenty-seven years old in 1963. FBI agents had questioned him about the two white men seen by Lay near the church on September 2. He told them he had not been able to recognize anyone in the car because of the shadow cast by the mimosa tree. He said he couldn't tell if the men were black or white. He had told agents that he had just arrived at the church area. It was interesting to Eddy that Captain Lay, in his statement, had said he asked White if he was with the two white men. But White had denied it, saying he had arrived at the church that night because he lived next door, renting a room in a boarding house.

The FBI had focused more than a little attention on White after the church was bombed. He told agents he had worked late the night before, playing music at a record party in Leeds, a town about twenty miles east of Birmingham. He said he had returned home late and then, early on the morning of September 15, he had walked to the Gaston Motel, about two blocks away, to have breakfast. He talked to a number of people, he said. He told agents that at precisely 9:59 A.M.—twenty-three minutes before the bomb exploded at the church—he had left with a friend to go to Montgomery. He remembered the time, he said, because he'd heard it announced on the car radio. He and the friend went to visit a girlfriend of White's who attended Alabama State College in the Alabama capital. They arrived on the campus around noon, White said, and heard the news of the bombing on the radio. The girlfriend, Connie McLarty, later told the FBI that White's visit was "completely unexpected."

Eddy did not know if the FBI viewed White as a suspect, or simply followed out every trail it could find. He located White, who said he would testify to what he saw if the case ever came to trial. It would be supportive testimony—assuming that Baxley could convince Captain Lay to be a witness and tell what he saw.

10

Eddy came across medical reports on the four girls who died in the blast. All four had been taken to University Hospital, which, in 1963, was still referred to by many as Hillman Hospital or Hillman Infirmary. A doctor had examined the bodies and pronounced all four girls dead. Someone had scrawled a "DOA" on Cynthia Wesley's report and noted that death was due to "decapitation." The Jefferson County coroner, J. O. Butler, had arrived shortly after and prepared the official death certificates:

> to certify the death of Denise McNair (c) who came to her death September 15, 1963, and was dead on arrival at the Hillman Hospital, Birmingham, Alabama, that she came to her death from a bomb blast at the Sixteenth Street Baptist Church, Birmingham, Alabama, by person or persons unknown, same being homicide.

> to certify the death of Cynthia Wesley (c) . . . and that she came to her death from a bomb blast at the Sixteenth Street Baptist Church, Birmingham, Alabama, by person or persons unknown, same being homicide.

> to certify the death of Carol [sic] Robertson (c) . . . and that she came to her death from a bomb blast at the Sixteenth Street Baptist Church, Birmingham, Alabama, by person or persons unknown, same being homicide.

to certify the death of Addie Mae Collins (c) . . . and that she came to her death from injuries received from a bomb blast at the Sixteenth Street Baptist Church, Birmingham, Alabama, by person or persons unknown, same being homicide.

The death certificates filled out by Butler on September 15, 1963, revealed that three of the girls had been born within twelve days of each other: Addie Collins had been born on April 18, 1949; Carole Robertson was born on April 24, 1949, and Cynthia Wesley* on April 30, 1949.

One Sunday morning, before the sun rose, Eddy woke up with the bombing on his mind and decided to go visit the Sixteenth Street Baptist Church. He parked a block or so away on Sixth Avenue—"I didn't want to alarm anyone," he said later. "I just wanted to be there."

The front of the church is actually on Sixth Avenue rather than Sixteenth Street, with three archways at the entrance. On that Sunday morning Eddy watched people arrive for church, park their cars, and walk to the front. It must have been something like that on the day of the bombing, he mused—old men in their brown or dark blue suits and shined shoes, shaking hands with fellow members; women in hats and high-heeled shoes; little boys looking uncomfortable in their shirts and ties; girls in their immaculate dresses, laughing and giggling in little clusters.

Later, after the services, he walked into the church and looked around. High above the front entrance was a magnificent stained-glass window depicting a black Jesus. It was a gift from the people of Wales. At the front, just to the right of the altar, enshrined in the wall, were pictures of the four girls who had been killed that day: Denise McNair, the youngest, with her slightly upturned nose and

*Cynthia Wesley was born Cynthia Diana Morris. Her natural parents were Estelle Merchant Morris and Charlie Morris; Mrs. Morris had seven other children. The Wesleys informally adopted Cynthia in 1955.

sparkling eyes, and Carole Robertson, Cynthia Wesley, and Addie Mae Collins, all of them smiling. Under the pictures were the words: *Their lives were taken by unknown parties on September 15, 1963, when the Sixteenth Street Baptist Church was bombed. May men learn to replace bitterness and violence with love and understanding.*

In his requests for reports on FBI interviews, Eddy was looking for material on all the Birmingham bombings, not just the bombing on the Sixteenth Street Baptist Church. The wide search was based on the assumption that most of the bombings and terror tactics were the work of a small band of klansmen, with most members of the group knowing something about all or most of the bombings. Baxley hoped that Eddy might find any case in which a klansman or former klansman could be indicted and brought to trial. Then, Baxley could offer immunity or reduced charges in exchange for information the suspect might have on the bombing that killed the four girls, a tactic known as getting a suspect to "flip."

Assistant Attorney General John Yung had found a nineteenth-century Alabama law that could be used to prosecute the bombing of a church or any other building, whether it caused a death or not. The law, which was not restricted by a statute of limitations, opened the way to bring an accused bomber to court if an explosive had been detonated near an occupied dwelling:

> Any person who willfully sets off or explodes any dy-
> namite or other explosive in, under, or dangerously
> near to any steamboat or vessel or railroad car in
> which there is at the time any human being, or any
> prison or jail or any other house or building which is
> occupied by a person lodged there in or any inhabited
> dwelling house or any house adjoining such house
> whether there is at the time in such house adjoining a
> dwelling house a human being or not, shall on con-
> viction be punished at the discretion of the jury by

death or by imprisonment in the penitentiary for not less than ten years.

In the five years from 1963 through 1968, the federal government pursued the bombing case as a civil rights violation, as there was no federal statute involving murder except on federal property. Under Title 18, Section 241, of the U.S. Code, a person convicted of violating the civil rights of another could be sentenced to a maximum of life in prison if the act resulted in death.

From April 26, 1956 through early September of 1963 there had been at least twenty racially motivated bombings and attempted bombings in Birmingham, none of which had been solved. Some had caused some minor injuries, but nobody had been killed. State officials at the time had repeated over and over, "But nobody's been killed. It's just an effort to *scare* the Negroes."

The rationale seemed to be that as long as no one was killed it wasn't worth a lot of effort to try to solve the cases. Bombings first rocked Birmingham in the 1940s, when blacks began moving into a previously all-white neighborhood along Center Street in the city's north side—which soon came to be known as "Dynamite Hill." But Eddy's investigation into bombing incidents was bracketed by the period 1956 through 1963, that span of time when the civil rights movement was in full swing and klan reaction became more flagrant. The bombing of the Sixteenth Street Baptist Church stood out for several reasons—the first being, of course, that it was not just a terror tactic but a homicidal event. Also, the amount of explosives used at the church was far greater than at other targets. For instance, when the New Bethel Baptist Church was bombed on January 16, 1962, there was only one stick of dynamite used. There were six sticks used at Bethel Baptist Church when it was bombed on December 14, 1962, slightly injuring two infants. Six sticks were also used at the Gaston Motel and at the residence of King's brother, A. D. King, both of which were bombed on May 11, 1963.

By Person or Persons Unknown

The home of attorney Shores was bombed twice within a two-week period in 1963, with two sticks of dynamite used in each case. But at the Sixteenth Street Baptist Church, between ten and twenty sticks of dynamite were detonated, and when they went off they did more than just scare people.

11

Birmingham police, especially Captain Jack LeGrand, strongly believed that the church bombing, and possibly other bombings, had been carried out by FBI informant Gary Thomas Rowe, whose undercover name was "Karl Kross." LeGrand and Sergeant Earnest Cantrell had branded Rowe as a liar who had stirred up klan violence in the 1960s to collect a fee from the FBI for reporting the activity. LeGrand and Cantrell believed the FBI may have covered for Rowe in cases where he might have done more than observe klan activity. LeGrand also believed that one of the department's patrol officers, LaVaughn Coleman, may have been an accomplice. Rowe had often ridden with Coleman on patrol during the 1960s. In the 1970s Coleman had refused to take a polygraph test in connection with the department's investigation; in 1977 he resigned from the force.

In reading Rowe's handwritten reports to the FBI in the early 1960s, Eddy noticed statements that were not consistent with what Rowe wrote in 1976 in his autobiography, *My Undercover Years with the Ku Klux Klan,* published by Bantam. Eddy asked Baxley about arranging an interview with the former FBI informant.

Rowe's name was linked in one way or another to many ugly incidents during the civil rights movement. Just ten days after the bombing of the church, another explosion—the "shrapnel bomb"—rocked Birmingham. The shrapnel bomb was actually the second of two explosions in the incident; the first went off in the street, and then ten minutes later came the explosion of a second, much more deadly bomb, which apparently had been set off by the klan to kill or maim officers responding to the first call. The second bomb contained the shrapnel—hammer claws, nails, and assorted iron and steel fragments. When officers arrived they found Rowe nearby making a telephone call; no one had asked him why he was there.

Back in 1961, when the Freedom Riders had come to Birmingham on Mother's Day, Rowe had been in the klan mob that attacked the group of integrationists. Later that same day he attacked a black man along a downtown street; the man pulled a knife and cut Rowe's throat. Klan members took Rowe to a hospital for emergency treatment.

Yet it was Rowe who broke the case following the 1965 march from Selma to Montgomery when a white woman from Detroit, Viola Liuzzo, had been shot to death by klan nightriders along U.S. 80. The shots had been fired from the car in which Rowe was riding; he eventually led agents to the other three men in the car, and it was his testimony that convicted Collie Leroy Wilkins, E. O. Eaton, and Eugene Thomas in a federal trial, which marked the first time whites were convicted of a racially motivated crime in Alabama.

Baxley, who had talked with Rowe earlier in the probe, arranged an interview. Rowe agreed to meet with Eddy and Birmingham police officers in San Diego, at the office of his attorney, Frank Geerdes. LeGrand and Cantrell accompanied Eddy. Under the federal witness protection program, Rowe, using different names, had lived in Georgia and California.

The main reason Eddy wanted a face-to-face interview with Rowe was to ask him about a statement by former klansman Robert Chambliss. Chambliss, who had been arrested in 1963 for possession of dynamite two weeks after the church bombing, had told a Birmingham police detective in 1975 that he had obtained dynamite prior to the bombing and had given it to "Rowe and them."

Eddy was told by Birmingham officers LeGrand and

Cantrell that they had been visited by Chambliss one afternoon in 1976. They said the former klansman had told them then that he just wanted to talk in general. Another officer, Captain Bill Myers, was also in the room. They said Chambliss rambled in his talk, then suddenly, on his own, told them that he knew about making a bomb—a bomb that would detonate when water dripping from a bucket with a hole in it changed the level of a fishing bobber attached to the triggering mechanism.

When Eddy, LeGrand, and Cantrell arrived at Geerdes's office Rowe was already there, waiting in the conference room. He was of medium height, with a bullish chest—he had once worked as a bouncer in a bar, and he looked the part. His reddish hair was close-cropped, his face square, the eyes narrow. He sat near the end of a long table in the attorney's conference room, by a tape recorder; he kept his hands clasped together, staring evenly at Eddy. Eddy's first question was about a man in a KKK unit, called a klavern. "On February 6, 1964, you told the FBI that you got some blasting caps from a subject named James Moore in the Warrior klavern. Do you remember that?"

Rowe nodded. "Yes, that's right."

"The FBI says there was never a subject by the name of James Moore in the Warrior klavern."

Rowe shrugged. "Well, that's who he was."

"They say there's no such person," Eddy said. "Now, why did you tell them—"

"Now, that's what I'm fixing to ask you," Rowe interrupted. "Now, why in the hell would I think up a James Moore?"

"I don't know. I'm just saying what you said. Nowhere in your file—"

"Hey, let me put it this way, okay?" Rowe injected, his voice testy, "because I see what you're trying to do."

"I'm only going where the record leads," Eddy said.

"That's right," Rowe said. "That's exactly what you've got."

Rowe claimed that it was he who had notified the FBI that the church had been bombed. He said a woman friend who worked for the Birmingham Police Department, Mary Lois McCord, had called him, and he had then called the FBI. The FBI files had it the other way around, with agents hurriedly calling Rowe.

"Here's what the FBI has recorded in their file," Eddy said. "[FBI Agent] McFall says that he contacted you at 9 A.M. that morning at your home. You asked him about an explosion that happened sometime around 4 A.M. that morning. You heard that explosion but you didn't know what it was. The agent checked and called you back at 9:30 A.M. and informed you that it was an industrial explosion. Then he hung up, and he called you back."

Rowe looked at him in puzzlement. "On the church bombing? That's not true."

"Let me tell you what they said happened that morning," Eddy said.

Rowe shrugged. "You got me now where I can just tell you, 'Hell no, go ahead.'"

Eddy said, "The agent called you about 10:25 A.M. after the church bomb and asked you—told you about it and asked you for suspects, and you told him Cagle, Keith, Hall, White, and maybe Thompson—because they were riding together was the reason that you gave him, that, those would-be suspects."

"I think I did name some of those names," Rowe said, "but that was just within minutes after they called me."

"Are you saying—"

"I'm saying I called the Bureau," Rowe said emphatically. "Mary McCord called me. And I called the Bureau."

"The records of the Birmingham Police Department show that Mary McCord did not work that day at all," Eddy said.

His eyes narrowed just a bit. "Mary McCord called me."

"They said she wasn't there that day," Eddy repeated.

"Then they're bullshitting you," Rowe said. "Call an ace an ace, you know. Mary Lois McCord called me, told me that it went down, was glad I was there [meaning at home]. I called the Bureau."

Eddy brought up the subject that had inspired the interview: "Chambliss, Bob Chambliss, had made the statement recently that he gave the ingredients of the bomb, the Sixteenth Street bomb, to 'Rowe and them.' You know why he would say that?"

"No."

"Other than the obvious, do you know why he would say that?"

"No sir."

"Why would he implicate himself by saying he gave the ingredients to you?" Eddy asked.

Rowe started to bristle. "I don't know, but if he had, goddamn, you would have already known about it, I can tell you that."

Eddy continued, "The reason I wanted you to reflect on that—"

"I don't have to reflect," Rowe snapped. "I can just flat-ass tell you."

"Obviously, I know what you're saying, but he obviously in making that statement has put himself in it," Eddy said.

"Then you better have his head shaved," Rowe snorted, "because he ain't too goddamn bright."

"I'm wondering why he would implicate himself," Eddy pressed.

"I'll be damned if I know," he said. "It's telling me he ain't too goddamn bright. To be honest with you, that was a stupid, dumb statement, okay? That's all I can say to that one."

"Okay," Eddy said.

"But I would like very much for you to ask me that on the poly, clear it up."

"Yes. I just wonder if you had some reflection as to why he would—"

"I'm dumbfounded," Rowe injected.

"—why he would go to some extreme to implicate himself to get you," Eddy said. "I can understand going to any other extreme."

Rowe shook his head. He said that in his opinion the case was going nowhere, that too much time had passed.

"I think right now what this room is doing is politicking. Now, I believe that in my heart. I might as well be honest with you, okay? I don't think there will ever be any indictments on that bombing. I've said that before, and I say it now."

At the end of the interviews, Eddy returned to Alabama, and in a memo to Baxley he wrote of Rowe: "In trying to reach some reason as to why an informer could be associated with the persons listed as the suspects that bombed the church and also suspects in other bombings . . . and never furnished any evidence against these individuals, leaves me with the conclusion he was a part of some of the bombings."

12

——
——
——

The FBI had, almost from the first, suspected three Ku Klux Klansmen as the ones directly responsible for the bombing and had compiled a list of other KKK members who might have been involved in the conspiracy to bomb the church.

The first suspect was Robert Edward Chambliss, age fifty-nine in 1963, a truck driver who had first joined the KKK in 1924. The second was twenty-five-year-old Thomas Edwin Blanton, Jr., who owned a 1957 Chevrolet, white over light blue or green, which had a whip antenna on the back. The third suspect, Troy Ingram, who was forty-five in 1963, had died in 1976, several months before Eddy was assigned to the case. Ingram had been a coal mine operator and, in 1963, had owned an auto-repair garage behind his home. He was also an electrician. The FBI had theorized that the bomb had been fabricated at Ingram's home.

The lists of possible conspiracy suspects included just about every known klan member in Birmingham: John Wesley Hall, Charles Cagle, Ross Keith, brothers Herman and Jack Cash, Bobby Frank Cherry, Earl Thompson, and a man called "Sister" White.

In an FBI report, Eddy read about several bystanders who said that just seconds after the explosion they saw two white men running away from the area of the church. One, they said, who appeared to run with a limp, was being helped by the other. Eddy came across reports in which agents speculated that the one with the limp might have been Troy Ingram, who had suffered a broken toe in August 1963. A doctor told the FBI that a broken toe could cause a person to hobble while attempting to run. But after looking at photographs, none of the witnesses could say positively that it was Ingram. They could only say that the man they saw limping along looked like Ingram.

Eddy was puzzled over the two white men—who were they and why were they there that day? Perhaps they were vagrants who happened to be passing through the area and were in the alley near the church when the bomb detonated—a blast like that would have sent anyone running. Or, alternatively, they could indeed have been klansmen sent to investigate why the bomb had not exploded. He suspected that the klan had not meant to kill anyone and had planned for the bomb to go off during the night. When it didn't, some of them might have gone to the church hoping to defuse it; if so, they arrived moments too late.

Eddy found a statement made by a man identified as William A. Crain, with reference to Troy Ingram. In that statement, made November 18, 1963, Crain told the FBI:

> I have known Troy for many years and have been close to him since shortly before my daughter [Mary Lois] married his son [Samuel]. We have had a falling out but are friends again. I have known for a long time that Troy Ingram hates Negroes and that he has taken part in demonstrations. A year ago he tried to organize some groups to go to Mississippi during integration trouble over there. I have heard him and others talk about beating up Negroes with chains. They went different places and talked about fights.
>
> On Monday night Sept. 9, 1963, I went to my daughter's house to pick up some furniture she had borrowed. It was dark and Samuel Ingram had turned the lights on but Mary Lois had not come home from work. I sat in my car near Troy's garage. I heard Troy talking

with a man I know as Cotton Isbell and an older man who may be Isbell's father. They were sitting on the ground and I do not believe they knew I was in the car. These men were talking about 'Niggers' and calling them vulgar names and cursing them. They were talking about explosives but I did not hear them say what they were going to use them for. I heard Troy say he had 12 to 15 sticks of dynamite in the garage. He took his flashlight and went into the garage. He came back in a few minutes and said, 'O.K. I've got enough.' I have heard Troy several times say he can get as much dynamite as he wants. He used to be a coal miner and used dynamite. I have seen Troy Ingram and Robert Chambliss visiting each other on a number of occasions and I know they are close friends.

Near the end of the statement Crain said, "Since the 16th Street Baptist Church was bombed on Sept. 15, 1963, I have heard Troy Ingram say that the only thing wrong was that they didn't kill all the 'Black——.'"

The statement was made to agents F. Willard Ralston of Little Rock, Arkansas, and Timothy Casey of Memphis. The two agents later questioned the man Crain had called Cotton Isbell—whom they identified as Carey Lee Isbell—who denied that he and Ingram had talked about beating blacks. He also denied that Ingram had told him he had made bombs. Isbell denied that he had taken part in any bombings. Later, Ingram told agents that Crain would make statements about him because Ingram had "beaten up" Crain over a problem involving their children.

A witness told the FBI that on September 4, 1963, he had observed Thomas Blanton remove a cardboard box about eighteen inches long from a shack at the rear of his house and put the box in the trunk of his car. That night Shores's home was bombed. Neither the witness nor the FBI had any idea what was in the box, but Blanton's actions that day seemed strange—apparently, Blanton's eighty-year-old father, Thomas E. Blanton, Sr., known as Pops Blanton, had been stopped by Birmingham police just as he left his house on Princeton Avenue. As the police talked with the elder Blanton just a block or so from the house, the younger Blanton screeched his car to a halt in the driveway, jumped out, removed the box from the little building behind the house, placed it in his car, and sped off, away from where his father was being detained by police. He made no attempt to check on how his father was faring with the police. When the younger Blanton was questioned later about the box, he told the FBI it had contained "literature."

Blanton was interviewed repeatedly about his whereabouts the night of September 14 and 15, 1963. He said he had been on a date with Jean Casey, but recounted their date differently during different interviews. At first, in early October 1963, he told agents Frank B. Spencer and Hugh H. Smith that he had picked up Miss Casey at 6:30 P.M. and then had either gone to a drive-in theater or spent the evening "driving around." He said they had stopped at a restaurant called the Hickory Hut, in the Five Points West Shopping Center. In a second interview, he omitted the Hickory Hut and said he and Miss Casey had gone to Ed Salem's Drive-In, on the city's north side. He said he did not see anyone he knew. But in another interview he told agents that at Ed Salem's Drive-In he had talked with Mary Lou Holt, the wife of klan member Bill Holt.

Blanton emphatically denied that he had anything to do with the bombing and said he had not driven by the church the morning of September 15. He denied that he and Miss Casey had concocted the story of his whereabouts that night. In one FBI report, Blanton appeared to be cooperating with agents, telling them of a September 4 meeting with Chambliss during which the subject of bombs came up:

Blanton stated that during the meeting Robert Chambliss got him to the side and stated to Blanton that he, Chambliss, was going to make a bomb that would throw metal. Blanton stated that he had had this information since he heard of the shrapnel bomb which was exploded September 25, 1963. He stated this information has been tearing him up inside and he has been afraid to tell anyone. Blanton advised that Chambliss actually wanted him to help make the bombs but he denied categorically any participation in making such a bomb.

But later in the same interview Blanton denied making any such statement, saying the agents must have misunderstood. He also denied being a member of the KKK but later recanted, saying he had belonged to the klan. At one point he told agents that he was against bombings of any sort: "Although he is a segregationist, he is against killing such as occurred as a result of the bombing of the 16th Street Baptist Church. Blanton said that if he knew the identity of the person or persons responsible for the bombing of the church, he would identify them without hesitation."

During one of the interviews Blanton was arrested—he allegedly took a swing at agent Bernard W. Cashdollar. Agents John F. McCormack and Joseph Zimmerman said they restrained Blanton, who then reached into his pocket. Agents said they trapped his hand and later removed a pocket knife. Blanton was arrested and jailed under $5,000 bond. Jefferson County Sheriff Mel Bailey agreed to have one of his deputies, J. C. Williams, pose as a car thief in the same cell, but Blanton told Williams nothing. Blanton was released on bond, and a federal grand jury later refused to indict him on a charge of assaulting a federal officer.

One of the first issues Eddy tried to resolve was the Chevrolet with the Confederate flag attached to its radio aerial, which many church members had seen the morning of September 15. It could have been the car that belonged to Blanton, Jr., Eddy believed, which was a white-topped 1957 Chevrolet with a blue bottom, though witnesses had variously described the car on the scene as "sea-blue," "green," or "turquoise." But the obvious reason the FBI believed the car might have been Blanton's was the whip antenna with a Confederate flag attached to it. Many white persons in the early 1960s had such flags attached to their cars, but it appeared more than coincidence that this would be a Chevrolet with the long radio aerial. Blanton's story was that he was at home sleeping and didn't get up until 11 A.M. He said he never went downtown that morning and did not drive by the church. But the FBI could never get a positive identification on the car, and none of Blanton's neighbors could say that they saw him leave the house that Sunday morning. They could not remember if the car was gone or there at his house.

ENOUGH STUFF TO FLATTEN
HALF OF BIRMINGHAM

13

The more Eddy read in FBI and police documents, the more convinced he became that the central figure in the bombings in Birmingham had been Robert Edward Chambliss, a former city employee and truck driver for a Birmingham auto parts dealer who, in 1977, was retired. In 1963 he had been fifty-nine years old. The FBI had repeatedly interviewed him, finding him openly hostile at some times, cooperative and even amiable at other times. He readily admitted that he did not like blacks or Roman Catholics of any color but said he had left the Ku Klux Klan in 1951, a statement that was untrue.

His history of violent klan activity was documented back into the 1940s, when Chambliss and two or three other klansmen had formed a "hit squad" that regularly went on "whipping forays," beating blacks who were moving into the Center Street neighborhood of the city. Not only had there been floggings of blacks, but a number of homes purchased by blacks had been bombed. Even back then Chambliss had been a target of police investigations, though he was never prosecuted for a felony. He did, however, stand trial on a misdemeanor charge for one of the beatings and was found guilty.

On October 1, 1963, just two weeks after the bombing, FBI agents Bernard Cashdollar and Timothy M. Casey, Jr., interviewed Chambliss:

Chambliss stated he dropped his affiliation with the klan at this time [1951] due to the unfavorable publicity which had been afforded him . . . particularly one incident for which he got an unusual amount of publicity involving the forcing of a Negro couple to move from a formerly all-white neighborhood. He stated at the time of this incident he was employed by the Department of Street and Sanitation of the City of Birmingham and because of this unfavorable publicity was fired. . . . He stated he felt this action by city officials was unfair as he had been only doing what he was told to do by Bull Connor, Birmingham Police Commissioner, but that Connor had failed to intercede for him at the time and he was fired outright. He stated it was his personal belief that the more recent bombings are committed by Negroes who are interested in building up sympathy for their cause and to make effective solicitation of money easier. He told the agents he felt the blacks hoped bombings would lead to riots which, in turn, would lead to federal troops being deployed in Birmingham, which would force integration.

A few weeks later, on October 29, Chambliss exploded when agents went to his place of employment at Rebuilt Auto Parts Company:

Chambliss showed a hostile attitude, and called for his employers, Mr. and Mrs. Herman Siegal, to come to the loading dock so they could witness him tell off the investigating agents. Mr. and Mrs. Siegal and two unidentified Negroes witnessed the remainder of the interview.

Chambliss stated, "I am going to tell the FBI where they can go. Seventy-two percent of the bastards are Roman Catholics under the control of that yellow traitor Bobby Kennedy, and they had better leave me alone. Now I am going to tell you. Stay away from my house and don't talk to my wife and relatives any more about me. I am warning you. I am going to sue you; you are trying to drive me crazy."

As he spoke, Chambliss was wildly waving his hands in the direction of the agents and pointing his finger at them, but he did not approach them. "Agent Cashdollar reminded Chambliss that if he had nothing to hide, there could be no logical reason for his present wild attitude, and that he was not acting like an innocent man," the report said.

The agents had told him they would continue their investigation with or without his approval, but they later did ask that he cooperate: "Chambliss did not orally acknowledge these statements, but appeared to be embarrassed that neither his audience or the interviewing agents had been impressed by his crude remarks."

Chambliss had made at least two statements concerning dynamite. In 1975 he told the Birmingham police that he had obtained dynamite prior to the bombing of the church and had given it to "Rowe and them." And back in 1963 he had told the FBI that he had indeed purchased dynamite on September 4, to be used to "clear stumps" from property on which the KKK had planned to build a clubhouse.

He had reportedly denied any knowledge of the church bombing. On September 29, 1963, he told Alabama State Highway Patrol Major Bill Jones that he didn't remember where he was the Saturday night before the church was bombed. "I was at home when it happened, I reckon." In that same statement he denied knowing anything about the other Birmingham bombings and denied belonging to the klan: "I did [belong] about 10 or 12 years ago. I got out to keep out of trouble. I still go to the open meetings, I believe in the klan."

Chambliss was a volatile man, at times erupting with temper. At other times, however, he seemed docile, almost serene, like a little boy, as he sat still for his wife, Flora Lee, known as "Tee," to comb his hair. He and Tee had something of a ritual; whenever Chambliss was going somewhere, he would ask her to comb his hair. In a statement to the FBI Mrs. Chambliss told of a 1965 occasion when Chambliss had to get up at 3 A.M. to carry auto parts to south Alabama. Mrs. Chambliss had awakened early, fixed coffee, and carried a cup to him. As he sipped it she stood behind his chair and combed his hair. He left the house a short time later, bidding her to go back to bed and turn out the light. Twenty minutes after he was gone, she said, she heard an explosion.

Flora Chambliss had a sister named Viola Hillhouse, who told Eddy her husband had belonged to the klan in 1948 and used to go to meetings with Chambliss. But apparently there was a falling out between the two men; one day, Mrs. Hillhouse said, her husband told her to take his KKK robe back to Chambliss. She took the robe to her sister's house and told Flora to give it to Chambliss. Later, she said, Chambliss smeared blood on the robe and took it to the Jefferson County Sheriff's Department. He told lawmen that Mr. Hillhouse had killed a Negro and dropped his body in a mine shaft. Although it wasn't clear that such a murder had occurred, officers questioned Hillhouse, who became angry. One day he called his wife at home and told her to leave the house; he was coming home to get his gun, he said, to kill Chambliss. But other relatives had intervened and the confrontation was avoided.

Eddy found that the FBI had suspected Chambliss in a number of bombings, including the shrapnel bombing ten days after the church bombing; amidst the debris of that incident agents had found a clutch plate that was apparently packed in as part of the explosive. The plate was identified as coming from a Hudson car made between 1940 and 1942. Although exhaustive follow-ups failed to show where it had come from, agents did locate a junkyard in Tallassee, Alabama, about a hundred and thirty miles southeast of Birmingham, which was part of Chambliss's regular route as a truck driver for an auto parts store in Birmingham; the owner of the yard thought he remembered Chambliss picking up such a clutch plate and getting it on his truck. But he wasn't positive.

Eddy interviewed a man named William Tallent, who had joined the klan in 1947; Tallent said Chambliss had been among the klansmen who belonged to an action group known as the Klokan. He said at regular klan meetings there was never any talk of violence, but after the meetings members of the Klokan would adjourn to a separate meeting room. In 1949, he said, members of the Klokan—including Chambliss—were indicted in connection with various floggings in the Birmingham area. Tallent had told the FBI that on August 12, 1949, the home of E. B. Deyanpert, a black man, had been bombed, and the five men who had thrown the bomb had been fired upon by Deyanpert, who apparently was not intimidated by klan terror tactics. Later, Tallent said, Chambliss was seen in a restaurant, laughing and bragging that he had been shot at. Tallent said he didn't know if Chambliss and the others had actually bombed the house, though it seemed possible that they had. On another occasion, April 22, 1950, the home of a black man named Benjamin W. Henderson was set afire, and Tallent recalled Chambliss bragging, "I like to play with matches."

Tallent said he had quit the klan in 1957 because the membership rolls swelled to include a large group of men from Anniston, a manufacturing city about sixty miles east of Birmingham; the Anniston men, Tallent recalled, were always armed.

On October 24, 1977, Eddy interviewed a minister who had pastored the 35th Avenue Baptist Church in 1955. The Reverend Harry W. Bentley recalled that Chambliss had been a member of the church. One day in 1955, Bentley said, he was speaking from the pulpit and telling the congregation of the favorable response he had received that week when he had spoken at a black church, the Sixteenth Street Baptist Church. Bentley recalled that Chambliss had abruptly stood up and walked out, a look of anger on his face. The next night, Bentley said, he was visited at home by Chambliss and three other men who asked him if he were a communist.

"Why do you ask?" Bentley had inquired.

"Well, you were preaching at the Sixteenth Street Baptist Church," one of the men had said.

Bentley recalled that he had replied, "The great commission tells me to go and preach the gospel."

"Do you have a communist card?"

"No. But I preach in jails, on street corners, at churches, and the Sixteenth Street Baptist Church," he had told them.

One of the men said they were interested in seeing to it that the 35th Avenue Baptist Church "got the right type of preaching." Bentley had responded by asking, "What church do you belong to?"

The pastor's wife, meanwhile, called some of the men of the church and several arrived, including Orr C. Pass, a deacon who also was the employer of Chambliss. A short time later the four men left, and Chambliss never returned to the church.

Long before Martin Luther King, Jr., or the Freedom Riders had come along, Chambliss's temper had become well known in Birmingham. One story has it that in 1949 he blew up at a klan rally in a rural section of Jefferson County. *The Birmingham Post* had sent two reporters to cover the rally, Clarke Stallworth, Jr., and George Cook. As the cross was lighted, Cook took a picture of Chambliss and other klansmen; Chambliss had lunged forward, cursing and swinging, knocking the flash unit from the camera. It fell smashed to the ground.

Stallworth and Cook were sitting on the hood of a car, watching a ring of robed klansmen surround them, muttering dire warnings. Just when the situation seemed about to explode a young klansman, barely more than a teenager, walked to the newsmen and said, "Hey look. Y'all have gotten some pictures and y'all got some notes. Now these guys over here are saying they're going to do some bad things to you. So why don't y'all just leave now."

Stallworth and Cook exchanged glances, and Stallworth remarked, "Well, maybe he's right. We've probably got what we came after." They beat a retreat. While Chambliss had ruined the flash unit he did not destroy the film in the camera, and the next day the newspaper published the picture. A short time later, Birmingham Mayor Cooper Green called Cook and Stallworth and asked them to come see him; when they arrived at city hall they found Chambliss, a city employee, in the mayor's office.

"Is this the man that broke your camera?" Green asked the reporters.

"That's him," Stallworth said.

Green pointed at Chambliss. "You either quit or be fired."

After that, Chambliss found jobs driving trucks and working at engine parts companies. But curiously, years later, when Stallworth again covered a klan meeting and a klan leader assured him he would be protected, one of those assigned to afford this protection was Robert Chambliss.

Mayor Green said in a statement to the FBI that Chambliss's behavior had been erratic and at times explosive. Green said that for two weeks after the firing Chambliss would drive his car to Green's house and park it there, sitting for hours and staring at the house. Green said his wife had become upset and frightened that Chambliss might try something. But Green said he never called for any police units to guard his home, and eventually Chambliss vacated his post in front of the house. Instead, he stayed in Green's neighborhood by day, telling residents who happened by that he needed their support and their signatures to get him hired again by the city of Birmingham.

14

There was a story among FBI agents that former klansman Earl Thompson was with Chambliss when the home of the Reverend Fred Shuttlesworth was bombed in 1958. The story went that Chambliss took the small charge of dynamite, got out of the car, and went to place the device near the house. Thompson and another man waited in the car, tense and sweating. Just then, a Birmingham police car turned onto the street and Thompson put his foot on the gas pedal, sending the car lurching forward. At the same time Chambliss, who was returning to the car as it started hurrying off, rushed to catch it. He managed to grab hold of the door handle and hang on as the car sped down the street. The ride scuffed the tops of his shoes away.

Eddy interviewed Thompson about that episode, but he said he didn't know anything about it, that he hadn't been there. Thompson was nervous. He had been questioned in the past by other investigators and it was clear he wished Eddy would go away. Thompson said he was a Christian now, that he had given up his past klan activity and was sorry he had ever gotten involved with the group.

"I never had anything to do with bombings, especially church bombings," he said.

Eddy pressed him about why he specified church bombings.

"I'll answer that question the same way every time," he said. "I had nothing to do with any bombings. But as far as segregation and what we called nigger-knocking goes, that was my specialty and I'll own up to that." He did admit being with Bobby Cherry, Bill Holt, and perhaps Troy Ingram when they tested a chemical capsule as a bomb detonator. But he repeated that he had not taken part in any bombings.

One of Eddy's first interviews was with a man named John Wesley Hall, a truck driver who had the peculiar nickname of "Nigger Hall." In 1963 he had been a member of the Eastview Klavern No. 13 of the United Klans of America, the same unit to which Chambliss belonged. On the day of the bombing, Hall had been questioned by FBI agents but insisted he knew nothing. Looking through the files, Eddy found that Hall had told the agents he feared for his life if he made any statements.

In another report Hall made a statement in which he said he had gone to the Chambliss home on the night of September 4 and 5, 1963, and was given a box of dynamite by Chambliss's wife. Hall said he and another klansman, a man named Charles Cagle, had carried the box to a field near Gardendale, a Birmingham suburb. Cagle later told Hall that the dynamite had been moved from the site and hidden elsewhere.

The FBI files included a report on polygraph tests taken by Hall: "It appears from this chart that Hall was attempting deception and he had knowledge of the 16th Street Baptist Church and may have participated in the bombing in some way or the planning thereof. At Hall's request, he was reinterviewed with the aid of the polygraph on Oct. 15, 1963. During this second interview, his reactions were substantially the same as those reported above."

Hall had been in the KKK when the Freedom Riders were attacked. In his statement to the FBI he had told of the ambush set up at the Trailways bus station in Birmingham. According to his statement, the klan "had a prior agreement with the Birmingham Police Department that there would be no interference by the Birmingham Police

Department with the attack by the klan on the Freedom Riders when they arrived. The agreement was that there would be approximately a fifteen minute delay."

Hall had also made a statement to the FBI that in 1963 Charles Cagle, Levi "Quickdraw" Yarbrough, and another man had burned a black church in Warrior, a community about 20 miles north of Birmingham. As the three men were preparing to burn the Warrior church, another group of klansmen went to a country fair nearby and attacked several blacks in the crowd, then ran away. While lawmen responded to a call about the disturbance, Hall and the others moved and set the church on fire.

George Beck, Baxley's chief deputy attorney general, came to Birmingham for the Hall interview. Hall was a large man with a dark complexion and dark hair, which probably accounted for his nickname. When Eddy told him he was investigating the church bombing, he nodded his head slowly.

"I already told the FBI everything I knew a long time ago," he said. "I don't really know that much."

Eddy nodded. "Well, looking at the FBI records it seems you know more than a little. We'd be interested in anything you have to say about it."

Hall let his eyes wander again, and rubbed an arm, thinking. Then: "I don't know. Maybe I'll have something to say to you later on. Maybe. I don't know."

Hall appeared shaky and nervous. He kept looking away, evading questions. Finally, he said he wanted to talk with his attorney. A few days later Eddy was called by Hall, who said he was at his attorney's office and would talk to him if he came there. Eddy hurried to the office, hoping he might be in for some solid information. But Hall was still edgy.

"I've thought about it," he said, "and I'm leaving to go to Florida tomorrow."

"Florida," Eddy repeated. "What for?"

"Vacation," he said.

"How long will you be gone?"

He shrugged. "Maybe a week or so, but when I get back I'll talk with you."

"Why don't we just talk now?" Eddy suggested.

"I'd rather wait until I get back," Hall said.

Eddy did not want to push him and have him back away. He felt Hall might be able to give new information on the case and might be a witness in the trial. From reading Hall's file, Eddy knew he could be helpful if he just repeated what he had said to the FBI back in the 1960s.

But a few days later Eddy received a telephone call from Sergeant Cantrell. "Bob, I know you had high hopes," Cantrell said, "but I got some bad news. Hall's dead."

Dead? Eddy was stunned. His first thought was that somehow the klan had found out he was going to talk and had killed him.

"What happened?" he asked.

"He died in Florida," Cantrell said. "They found him in a motel room. Apparently he died from cirrhosis of the liver. A member of the family called me a little while ago. They said he'd been sick."

Eddy hung up the telephone with a sense of dismay and disappointment. Hall was a man who was ready to talk, he believed. Neither Eddy nor the FBI thought Hall had been directly involved in the bombing of the church, though they believed he knew a lot about the other bombings. But it was all going to the grave with him. The first real lead had evaporated.

15

Eddy found a statement from an unnamed witness who had told the FBI that the klan had made plans to battle the 1963 school desegregation orders by setting fires in downtown buildings. While police officers and firemen would be busy there, the KKK planned to go to a high school and dynamite it. Apparently the plan was scuttled—and the Sixteenth Street Baptist Church targeted instead.

Some of the klan tactics might be considered comical had they not been so full of hatred. One klan member liked to put mustard gas in a syringe, which he carried into a store or other crowded public place. He would sidle up to a black person and quickly shoot the gas onto exposed skin, such as the neck or the arms or legs. Then he would move away. In a few moments the mustard gas would begin burning the victim and he or she would frantically search for water to cool the discomfort.

On one occasion in 1963, KKK members filled jars with fish, which they let rot for several days. Then they took the jars to Birmingham's Alabama Theater, which had agreed to desegregate. The klansmen went into the theater, set the jars under the seats, and unscrewed the lids. When the odor began to seep out, the audience evacuated.

As Eddy prepared to go out for an interview one day, FBI agent Cole Geary asked, "Where's your gun?"

Eddy looked at him. "I have it in my briefcase."

Geary shook his head like an angry bull, "You can't go out there and interview these people with no weapon on you."

"I'll be all right," Eddy said, laughing. "They won't bother someone with an office in the FBI building."

Geary didn't think it was funny. "You need to start carrying a gun."

Eddy had registered in his own name at the Holiday Inn and would end up staying there for ten months. It was inevitable that some of the klansmen or their supporters would find out where he was staying; after a few months he started getting calls.

A man said, "Are you that guy Baxley's got snooping around up here?"

Eddy said yes.

"Why don't you just leave the thing lie already, for God's sake?" the caller said.

"Why don't you meet me and we'll talk about it?" Eddy said.

The man hung up.

The only threatening call came from a woman who said he had better watch all sides when he left his room. She hung up hurriedly. He began to think about carrying the pistol but never did.

Eddy had learned about danger as a Marine in Korea in 1951, assigned to a recoilless rifle team. But in Korea, he had known who the enemy was and, usually, where the enemy was. Now, in dealing with the Ku Klux Klan, he didn't always know.

He had heard that a retired Birmingham police lieutenant, Maurice House, had handled many of the klan cases in the 1960s and had a headful of information. He went to see House one day, and as they talked House mentioned that Ross Keith might be of help in the investigation. Keith's name had appeared repeatedly in the FBI files.

"Will he talk to me?" Eddy asked.

"I think he will, but let me go see him first. It's been a while since I've talked with him."

A day later House called Eddy at the FBI office and said he had found Keith.

"Well, when can I see him?" Eddy asked.

"I don't know," House replied. "He's real sick. He's staying with a sister. I went over there and Keith said to give him a couple of days. I believe he has cirrhosis or something."

Eddy winced. Cirrhosis was what had killed John Wesley Hall. Eddy remembered reading an FBI statement by Hall in which Keith had been mentioned. On the morning of the bombing, Keith and Hall had been at a junkyard not far from downtown. When the blast went off, they stopped talking.

"What was that?" Hall had asked.

And Keith had laughed and replied, "Sounds to me like somebody's discriminating against the niggers."

Eddy would never get to talk to Keith. About a week later, House called to say he had died.

In late July Eddy spent an hour talking to a former Jefferson County Sheriff's Department investigator, James Hancock, who had spent much of his time working on bombing cases in the early 1960s. Hancock, now a private security guard, had little concrete information that Eddy could use. He did say he felt he had once been close to breaking the church bombing case and had even managed to place a "bug" in the home of Robert Chambliss. But the device had not produced useful information.

The next day Eddy wasted a morning going to Cullman, about forty miles north of Birmingham, to see if he could locate a former klansman called Sister White. A Cullman police lieutenant, Wendell Roden, rode with him to known and previous addresses, but the search came up empty.

This was getting to be a pattern, Eddy believed; again and again, he kept coming up empty. The original ninety-day assignment had long ago been extended indefinitely, and Eddy had now spent half a year on the church bombing case.

16
———
———
———

When Eddy arrived back at his office in the FBI building, he noticed two large files lying on his desk, apparently left by agent Geary. The folders contained interviews with relatives of Chambliss. His interest suddenly sharpened; he hadn't seen these files before.

One of the reports contained an interview with a woman named Elizabeth Hood, a niece of Flora Chambliss. She said that Chambliss once told his family to watch television that night, and later there was a bombing. She said that Chambliss's wife once scolded him by fussing that all the bombings had done nothing and desegregation was continuing in Birmingham. After the bombing of the Sixteenth Street Baptist Church, the statement by Miss Hood said, Chambliss quipped to his wife: "Is that big enough for you?"

Alarms went off in Eddy's brain. He read the rest of the day and long into the night. Elizabeth Hood had told the FBI a lot, quoting direct statements from Chambliss that could be damaging to him in a trial. One of the problems the FBI had had in the case was finding witnesses who would testify. Eddy felt sure that getting Elizabeth Hood to agree to testify had been a problem in 1963 and would be a problem now—if, in fact, he could ever find her. He went back to his motel room and called George Beck, going over Hood's statements with him. Beck was as excited as he was. "Where is she now?" he asked.

"I don't know," said Eddy, "but tomorrow I'll try to find her."

That same evening he called Captain LeGrand at home and asked for help in locating Elizabeth Hood for an interview. LeGrand said he would look into it. Next morning at the FBI office Eddy asked agent Geary if there were any more files on her; Geary found more and put them on Eddy's desk. They contained material that was even more dramatic than the first documents.

She had made a statement to the FBI on October 11, 1963, which read:

I, Elizabeth Hood, furnish the following information to [FBI Agent] Robert P. Womack freely and voluntarily. I have known Robert E. Chambliss all of my life as he is married to my mother's sister. During my adult life I have heard remarks from him and remarks from other members of the family which cause me to believe that he is definitely capable of acts of violence, particularly to members of the Negro race. On one occasion . . . I saw what Mrs. Chambliss said was dynamite and in another instance blasting caps. I recall that at about this time there was a bombing of a residence reported in the Fountain Heights area.

On September 14, 1963, I went by his house before 7:45 A.M. I related an incident about which I had read in the paper concerning a negro male stabbing or cutting the arm of a white girl who was the daughter of Birmingham police officer named Bieker. I also told him that Bob Gafford, a friend of the family, had offered a one hundred dollar reward leading to the arrest and conviction of this unknown negro. Chambliss became angry and during his profane outburst he said if Gafford could offer a one hundred dollar reward, he could offer a thousand. He then made comments concerning the negroes in general, and as best I can remember these comments were made by him. "You wait until after Sunday, they will beg us to let them segregate." He also said he had enough "stuff" put away to flatten half of Birmingham. During this conversation, he said he had been fighting a one-man war since World War II and if the boys would have helped him at all he would have been able to have accomplished considerably more. He commented during these remarks that he had learned the address of the "nigger" girl that was going to integrate the school. I commented to him that he should be careful not to do anything foolish, and he said he "would be in something he could get away in." The bombing of the Negro church occurred the following day.

I do not know of my own knowledge that Chambliss did or did not commit any of the bombings in the Birmingham area. [s] Elizabeth H. Hood.

At the end of the statement, the FBI noted that Hood advised them that she believed Chambliss was capable of bombing the Sixteenth Street Baptist Church and added that she was "convinced that he was closely associated with the bombing in Birmingham, Alabama, if not an actual participant."

In another FBI file was a statement from Hood that surprised Eddy. She said she "would not hesitate to testify to the above facts if she had some assurance that Chambliss would be convicted but would be reluctant to testify otherwise inasmuch as she, along with other members of her family, feared him." Further in the report, the FBI noted that Elizabeth Hood indicated that "she could not aptly express her complete distrust, dislike, and disgust at Chambliss and considered him to be devoid of compassion for anyone. She was of the opinion that each member of her mother's family felt the same way about Chambliss." She also said she believed Chambliss would not hesitate to seek revenge against her and would be "capable of planting a bomb in the middle of their house" to obtain revenge.

Prior to the event, she said, he had commented repeatedly, "We oughta blow that church up." After the bomb had exploded and it was reported on radio and television that four girls had been killed, Chambliss was heard to say, according to Hood's report, "We didn't mean to kill anybody" and "[i]t was supposed to have gone off earlier."

Eddy asked the Birmingham officers for help in locating Miss Hood. The next day Cantrell called Eddy to say he had located her and she was still in Birmingham. "Her name is Cobbs now," he said. "I told her to call you at the FBI office."

"Cobbs," Eddy repeated.

"She's a minister now," Cantrell added.

Eddy relayed the information to Baxley's office and was told that the attorney general and two assistants, George Beck and John Yung, would come to Birmingham the following day, hoping to talk with Elizabeth Hood Cobbs. Her statements about Chambliss were a revelation to Baxley.

That next morning Beck called to say Baxley would be at the Passport Inn that afternoon, and the meeting was set for five o'clock. Eddy still hadn't heard from Mrs. Cobbs and was concerned that she might not contact him. But shortly before noon the telephone rang. "Is this Bob?" asked a woman.

"Yes."

"I was told to call you. I'm Elizabeth Cobbs."

He thanked her for the call, and after a few preliminary remarks she asked why he wanted to talk to her. He told her it was about the church bombing; this information seemed to upset her. He then asked about talking with her in person.

"I'm planning to go on vacation," she said. "I'm leaving tomorrow. Couldn't all this wait until I return?"

Eddy said it couldn't. He told her Baxley was coming to Birmingham that afternoon. Then he asked, "Could you meet with the attorney general this afternoon around five?"

After a long pause she said she could, but that she wanted her husband to come to the meeting.

"That's fine," he said. He told her where Baxley and his assistants would be.

Enough Stuff to Flatten Half of Birmingham

That afternoon Eddy went to the Passport Inn; Baxley, Beck, and Yung were already there. A few minutes after five, Eddy responded to a knock on the door; a woman stood there, a man standing slightly behind her.

"Mr. Eddy?" When he nodded, she said, "I'm Elizabeth Cobbs."

He opened the door for her. She appeared nervous and was smoking a cigarette. As she and her husband entered, Baxley and his aides stood and shook hands with them. Mrs. Cobbs was an attractive woman who appeared to be in her mid-thirties. She wore slacks. Her hair was sandy and she wore glasses. She sat down and then quickly said, "I just want to know how you are going to involve me in this."

"We just need your help," Baxley said. "Just your cooperation."

"This has me very upset," she said. "I went through this with the FBI back when it happened."

"Four kids were killed," Baxley said.

"I know that," she said. "But what do you want from me? Just talking to you makes me nervous. All that is behind me. I feel that something could happen. Are you going to involve me?"

"We just need your help," Baxley repeated. He said nothing about asking her to testify in court. She smoked another cigarette. Her husband stood by, saying nothing. "I was just planning a nice vacation," she said. "And now this comes up. After all this time. I just don't know what to do."

Baxley asked some general questions about her statements made to the FBI, saying he wanted to go over them with her. She said she had to leave but would think about it. "I'll call Mr. Eddy when I get back," she volunteered.

"Bob, she's going to make a good witness," Baxley told Eddy after she left. "You gotta get her to testify. You've got to. She'll be a great witness." Then, almost as an aside, he declared, "She's a Methodist."

Eddy looked at him with surprise. "A Methodist? What's being a Methodist got to do with it?"

Baxley grinned, "Methodist ministers, Bob. They're well educated and they make excellent witnesses."

Eddy shrugged. "Well, my minister is an ordained minister and has his doctorate in divinity. And he's not a Methodist. He's a Baptist."

"Yeah, but not all Baptists are that well trained," Baxley shot back. "Methodists are."

"Methodists make better witnesses than Baptists?" Eddy asked. "Come on."

Then they all started laughing. It didn't matter. The enthusiasm that evening was like electricity. They were all talking at once, caught up for the first time since the probe started in a mood reflecting the possibility that they could win. Baxley was tugging at Eddy's sleeve—"Bob, you gotta keep after her. We need her as a witness. She can make this case. Keep after her."

Eddy nodded. "She's scared, you can tell that."

"You tell her we'll protect her," Baxley said. "She doesn't have to be afraid of Chambliss anymore, or of any other klansmen."

17

————
————
————

In early August 1977, just after the meeting with Mrs. Cobbs, Eddy found a report in the FBI files about a witness named Gertrude Glenn, also identified as Kirthus Glenn, a black woman who lived in Detroit. She had been visiting in Birmingham at the time of the bombing, staying with a friend who lived on Seventh Avenue North, just across the alley from the church. She told the FBI that she and a friend, Henry Smith, were returning to the house shortly after 2 A.M. on September 15. She said she noticed a car parked on Seventh Avenue North, about one block from the church. She said the car was a white-and-turquoise Chevrolet. Mrs. Glenn said she took note of the car because there were three white men in it, whom she described as middle-aged, wearing hats and short-sleeved shirts. An FBI document stated that Mrs. Glenn said she became "suspicious of the Chevrolet because of the fact that it contained three white men, that this particular area is occupied by members of the Negro race, and in addition, because of the late hour at which time the car was observed in the area."

The FBI had shown Mrs. Glenn thirty-four pictures of klan members and she had picked out three as resembling the men she had seen sitting in the car. All three pictures were different poses of one man—Robert Chambliss. Mrs. Glenn had also been shown photos of the car owned by Tommy Blanton, Jr., which she identified as the one she and Smith had seen.

Interestingly, Mrs. Glenn had contacted the FBI again after she had returned home to Detroit. In October 1963 she had seen a picture of Chambliss in a *Jet* magazine article about the charges of illegal possession of dynamite, and she had called the FBI office in Detroit, telling agents that the man in the picture looked like the man she had seen sitting in the car parked near the church early on the morning of September 15.

Baxley told Eddy to stay in Birmingham and continue his search for witnesses; he sent Shows and Yung to Detroit to visit Mrs. Glenn and ask her to testify. On August 17 they caught a plane to Detroit, rented a car, and went to Mrs. Glenn's home. She chatted amiably with the visitors from Alabama, and the meeting seemed to go well—so well that she invited them to stay for dinner, promising to cook them a steak. But she declined to come to Alabama and testify. Shows and Yung promised she would be protected, but she did not budge. The next day they returned to Montgomery, where Baxley did not appear particularly discouraged by their bad news. "I'll go up and talk to her myself," he said, and then told Shows to be prepared for another trip to Detroit. "We need her. She can put Chambliss there, and she can identify Blanton's car."

Several days later he and Shows caught a plane to Detroit; with them this time was Milton Belcher, one of the black attorneys on Baxley's staff. Shows made the introductions and Belcher made a pitch, saying the racial atmosphere in Alabama had changed. "Mrs. Glenn, we need your help to bring some klansmen to trial," he said. "You'll be protected." But Mrs. Glenn was unmoved; she did not want to return to Alabama to testify.

Baxley was buffaloed. As they drove back to the airport, however, he was struck with an idea—here they were in Detroit, which was now the home of Rosa Parks, the woman whose arrest on a Montgomery bus in 1955 had ignited the modern civil rights movement. She had moved to Detroit after the bus boycott.

"Why don't we go see Mrs. Parks and ask her to talk to

Mrs. Glenn?" he asked. There was no response. "I guess not," he said. "I don't know her. It wouldn't work."

But back in Montgomery he was hit by another idea—if he couldn't get Rosa Parks to intercede, he would get the attorney who had represented her in the bus case, Fred Gray of Tuskegee, one of the premier civil rights attorneys in Alabama. Baxley called him and asked for his assistance.

"I'll go with you," Gray said. "When do we go?"

A few days later they were back in Detroit, and Baxley introduced Gray as the man who had represented both Mrs. Parks and Martin Luther King, Jr. Mrs. Glenn listened as Gray told her about Baxley's efforts to bring justice in the bombing case. After about thirty minutes she said she'd do what she could to help. Shows told her, "Now the minute your plane lands in Birmingham, I'll be there with you. There will be others, too. We'll put you up in a motel, and I'll be right in the next room. If you hit the wall, I'll be there in a second."

Baxley told her Alabama would pay her expenses. Mrs. Glenn nodded and asked if she might bring along a friend, a woman who lived next door. "That's fine," said Shows.

18

————
————
————

On August 15, 1977, Elizabeth Cobbs called Eddy. She was back from vacation, she said, and in the midst of moving to a new apartment. She said she had a little time to talk; Eddy went to his car and fifteen minutes later was at her apartment in the northeast section of the city. Mrs. Cobbs opened the door, and he followed her into the kitchen, where the table and floor were covered with cardboard boxes and pots and pans. She was packing. She told him to sit down, and they talked while she continued her work with kitchen utensils and glassware.

As they talked and went over some of her statements, she told him about her uncle Robert Chambliss and what she had heard him say. She wasn't reading from a file but working on packing pots and pans as she related times and places of remarks made by Chambliss in her presence. Eddy was amazed at her memory; she could make an excellent witness. But then, as if she could read his mind, she announced, "I'm not going to testify."

She was still packing kitchenware when she told him that Gail Tarrant* might be of help.

Eddy nodded, as if he knew who Gail Tarrant was, which he did not. Because he was working out of the FBI office, people he interviewed often assumed that he was familiar with everything in the FBI's files—an assumption

———

*Gail Tarrant is the FBI's code name for an informant. Some documents refer to her as "Dale" Tarrant.

that sometimes worked in his favor. Now, trying to sound matter-of-fact, he said, "Tell me about you and Gail."

Mrs. Cobbs rattled pans around in a box, then announced, "I didn't go to the church that night. That's not true. She said that, and she later told me to back up her story to the FBI."

What night at the church? Mrs. Cobbs was telling Eddy something he knew nothing about. "Tell me about that," he said. Mrs. Cobbs nodded. She told him it was her understanding that Gail Tarrant had gone to the Sixteenth Street Baptist Church the night before the bombing and had seen klansmen there. Mrs. Cobbs said Gail had told the FBI the story, and she, Elizabeth Cobbs, had "backed it up," claiming to have been there, too.

The story she told was protected-source material that the FBI had not released to Eddy. He had never heard it before. Next day he went to agent Geary and asked about seeing the file on Gail Tarrant.

Geary paused. "Bob, this may be a problem. I'll have to see about it."

Several days went by. One morning Eddy found a file on his desk. An agent walked into the room behind him and said, in a hushed tone, "Bob, you've never seen that file." He then walked out. Eddy sat down and hurriedly opened the manila folder of documents dealing with Gail Tarrant.

About a year after the bombing, she had told the FBI that she and Elizabeth put on wigs and went to the church that night of September 14 and 15, 1963. They had been watching for Chambliss. Her story was that they saw Tommy Blanton, Jr., in his car, with Chambliss, Bobby Cherry, and another man whom they could not see clearly. She told the FBI that they watched as Cherry got out of the car, followed by Chambliss. Both men walked up the alley toward the church, Cherry carrying a small, weekend-style satchel in one hand. Chambliss then came back and got in the car, which headed north and made a right turn at the end of the block. Cherry continued walking up the alley.

She also said that after the bombing she heard Chambliss lament, "They're going to get me, Cherry, Blanton, and Cash." In another statement, she reported she had heard Chambliss say he watched while Cherry walked along the alley by the church, carrying the bomb.

Eddy repeatedly called Mrs. Cobbs, asking her to arrange a meeting with Gail Tarrant. She seemed hesitant at first but later agreed to locate her and pass along his request. Then one afternoon in late August Mrs. Cobbs called to say Gail had agreed to talk with him. The two women came to the motel that afternoon; their meeting lasted only a few minutes, during which Eddy went over some of the statements Gail had made thirteen years earlier to the FBI. She frequently answered a question with a question of her own—"Why don't you look in the FBI files for that?" or, "Didn't you already read that in my file?" Eddy believed she was trying to find out how much he knew.

A few days later he met with her again and zeroed in on her FBI statement about the night of September 14 and 15, 1963. "Why did you wait a year to tell the FBI that you had been there and seen that?" Eddy asked.

"I don't know." Then she shook her head. "But I wasn't there. I just said that."

"You weren't there?"

"No."

"Well, then how did you know that these men had been there and Cherry had placed the bomb?" he asked.

She told him she had "just put the pieces together." As a friend of Chambliss's wife, Tee, she said, she had often overheard Robert Chambliss making statements. The day before the bombing, she told Eddy, she heard Chambliss make a statement about "the meeting place where the niggers plan their marching." It wasn't the first time she had heard him berate that church, she said, and on occasions prior to September 15 she had believed he would bomb it.

Again, Eddy asked her, "Why did you wait a year before telling the FBI about this?"

"I told Deputy Hancock about it before it happened," she announced.

Eddy was stunned. She was talking about James Hancock, who had been an investigator for the Jefferson County Sheriff's Department in 1963. Eddy had already interviewed him but had learned nothing. "You told Hancock about this before the bomb exploded?" he asked.

"Yes, I did," she said. She told Eddy that she had been an informer for Hancock, and on the night of September 14 or early in the morning of September 15, 1963, she had called him at home to tell him about the klansmen. She said she had told Hancock that the bomb was down at the church.

"What did he say when you told him this?" Eddy asked.

"He hung up on me."

Eddy stared at her, puzzling over her words. She had told a law enforcement officer about a bomb at the church, and the officer had hung up? "Then what happened?" he asked.

"Well, next morning he called me, and I met him at about 8:30 over at Tarrant City." Tarrant is an industrial suburb about five miles north of downtown Birmingham.

"So you met him there at 8:30 and told him about the bomb?"

"Yes."

"And then what happened? What did he do?"

"Well, later he drove down there toward the church, but the bomb went off."

"If you told him about the bomb at 8:30 and the bomb didn't go off until about 10:20, what took so long?" he asked.

She was silent.

"Was there something going on between you two?" he asked.

She said nothing.

"That's why you won't testify," he said.

"I can't," she said. "I'll die before I hurt my family. My grandchildren will never be hurt because of what I saw or may have known."

"And Hancock never said anything about it to anyone?" Eddy asked.

"No, but a year later or so he took me to the FBI, and I told them."

"About you and Hancock?"

"No. I never told anyone that before," she said. "I told the FBI about seeing the men that night at the church and carrying the bomb."

Eddy contacted Hancock and asked him for another interview. Hancock, who was now working as a private security guard, agreed to meet Eddy the next night after work. When he arrived at the Holiday Inn, Eddy immediately confronted him with Gail Tarrant's assertion that she had told him the bomb had been placed at the church.

At first Hancock denied having heard from her. But then, after mulling it over, he told Eddy that he had indeed received a telephone call from an informer. He said the call had come at 10:15 A.M. on September 15, and he had rushed to the church; the bomb had gone off as he was driving, he said.

After further questioning, however, he admitted that he had met with Gail Tarrant that morning—briefly, he said— and then rushed to the church, too late.

"She says she told you about it two hours before it went off," Eddy said. "Why'd it take you two hours to respond?"

Hancock shrugged, "In those days there were false alarms every time I turned around. If I checked them all out, I'd have done nothing else."

Eddy reminded him that this information was not an anonymous bomb threat, but the word of a person he apparently knew quite well. Hancock said nothing. Then Eddy asked him again why he had taken so long to respond.

Hancock replied that there had been a "personal thing" between him and Gail Tarrant.

Eddy felt sick. Nothing about the case seemed more frustrating or agonizing—if Hancock had immediately gone to the church that morning, if he had just placed a telephone call, four young girls at the Sixteenth Street Baptist Church might not have been killed.

19

———
———
———

Former klan member Bobby Frank Cherry was located by Birmingham Police Sergeant Cantrell in Grand Prairie, Texas, a suburb of Dallas. Cherry was the man who, according to the statement made by Gail Tarrant, had been seen walking along the alley carrying the bomb the night of September 14 and 15, 1963.

Eddy caught a plane for Texas and arrived there on a glaring hot August morning. He had notified the Grand Prairie Police Department, which had already contacted Cherry and asked him to come to the police station. Cherry came voluntarily, though police had told him Eddy had a subpoena.

Cherry was forty-eight years old, a big man with thick, wavy, reddish hair. He had a down-home style of talk and expression, mixed with nervous laughter, that reminded Eddy of actor George Lindsay, better known as Goober on the Andy Griffith television show. Cherry seldom looked directly at Eddy but sat sideways in his chair, often leaning forward, his elbows on his knees.

After a few routine background questions, Eddy asked, "What do you know about the bombing of the church where the four girls were killed?"

Cherry shook his head. "Nothing. But I've been catching hell about it for years and never did a damn thing."

Then Eddy quickly announced: "Chambliss says he saw you walking down the alley and carrying the bomb to the church."

Cherry was jolted upright, his eyes wide. "Why did he say that about me? I didn't do it. Why'd he tell you that?"

"I don't know why," Eddy said. "That's just what he said. Said he saw you carry the bomb and walk down the alley to the church."

Cherry stared at the floor again. "I just don't believe he said that about me. I didn't have a thing to do with it."

Eddy questioned him about Chambliss. Cherry denied knowing him. But when shown statements he had made years earlier, he admitted that he and Chambliss had been friends. Eddy asked him about his alibi for the night of September 13, 1963, the night apparently that the bombing was planned. Cherry said that on that night he had been at a sign shop owned by Merle Snow. He said he and others were making placards and signs to protest blacks being admitted to West End High School.

"Mr. Snow can vouch for me," Cherry said.

"Mr. Snow's dead," Eddy replied. "Some of the other people deny seeing you there."

Looking troubled, Cherry leaned forward again, drawing deeply on a cigarette. "Sounds like someone's trying to put this on me," he said.

"It looks that way," Eddy said. He again asked him about the Sixteenth Street Baptist Church and being seen walking down the alley behind it carrying the bomb.

"How would you know if I walked down that alley?" Cherry asked.

"The only way I'd know it is if someone had said it," Eddy said. "How else would I know?"

Cherry shot a side glance at him. "I didn't do it," he said, and he would not budge from that story. The interview ended, with Eddy under the impression that Cherry looked shaken. Cherry later called the Grand Prairie Police Department from his home and said his stomach was so upset he couldn't eat or go to work.

Eddy, meanwhile, asked the Texas authorities if they could get a record of the phone calls Cherry made that night. Eddy figured Cherry would go straight home and call

Chambliss. He was nearly right. Cherry made three calls that night, all to Birmingham. But he didn't call Chambliss. One number he called belonged to Bob Gafford, a member of the Alabama legislature.

Late that night an angry Cherry called Eddy at the Grand Prairie motel. "Chambliss didn't tell you a damn thing," he snapped. "You lied to me. He didn't say a thing to you about that bombing."

"I didn't say he told me," Eddy said. "I said he had said that he saw you carrying the bomb down the alley—I didn't say who he had said it *to*. But that is what happened, isn't it?"

"I don't have to talk to you," Cherry muttered. "Chambliss's attorney said I didn't have to talk to anybody."

Eddy chuckled. "Is it always a good idea to listen to what somebody else's attorney tells you?"

There was a pause. And Cherry again laughed nervously. "I hadn't thought about that," he said, still chuckling.

Eddy made a final pitch for him to come to Alabama voluntarily and testify for the state. But Cherry said he was through talking.

It was an ironic twist that Cherry should have called Alabama Representative Bob Gafford. In 1963 Gafford had operated an auto parts business near the Chambliss home in Birmingham's northside; he and Chambliss were friends. Now, in 1977, Gafford was a member of the legislature of Alabama. When that body was in session in Montgomery, he sat next to a black legislator from Birmingham, Chris McNair, the father of Denise McNair, one of the four girls killed in the bombing.

Even before Eddy met with Elizabeth Cobbs or heard about Gail Tarrant, a special grand jury was impaneled in Birmingham to look into bombings that had occurred during the late 1950s and 1960s. Baxley had called it, hoping some of the former klansmen might decide to unburden their souls. Dozens of former KKK members were subpoenaed, including Robert Chambliss. On the first day of the session,

August 9, Eddy met with Baxley, Beck, and Yung, who were going to be in charge of the questioning. The Jefferson County Courthouse, a brown sandstone building, sat beside Woodrow Wilson Park, a stretch of green grass, trees, clean, wide sidewalks, flowers, and several long pools filled with big goldfish that swam in lazy circles. On a hot August day, it was a pleasant place to visit. The inside of the courthouse was not quite so pleasant. The corridor on the second floor was packed with former klansmen and their families and supporters. As he entered, Eddy heard catcalls and obscenities. While Beck and Yung were inside with the grand jury, Eddy sat on a bench at the far end of the hallway, trying to ignore the hostile stares and remarks.

Jefferson County Circuit Court Judge Robert Crowder walked into the hallway, past the crowd.

"I've never experienced such hatred before," Eddy told him.

"I'll tell you," Crowder said, "they'd better have something more than just the say-so of Gary Thomas Rowe. They'd better have some evidence."

The grand jury session lasted five days. Baxley obtained no solid evidence or witnesses and did not try for any indictments. But the tension seemed to get to Robert Chambliss. One day, in the courthouse corridor, a TV cameraman—a black man—was trying to shoot some footage; suddenly Chambliss leaped up and swung at him, knocking the camera to the floor. Deputy sheriffs rushed in.

20

Baxley believed that, without the testimony of Elizabeth Cobbs, he stood little chance of getting Chambliss convicted. In early September of 1977 he called Eddy and told him to press Mrs. Cobbs to agree to be a state's witness in the event Chambliss was indicted.

Eddy phoned her, saying it was urgent that they talk as soon as possible. After a moment's pause she agreed to meet him the following morning. When she came to Eddy's room in the Holiday Inn shortly after nine o'clock the next morning her face was set, her eyes hard and bright.

He immediately said, "I have to ask if you will testify to the things you have already told the FBI and told me."

She sat by the window and stared out, shaking her head slightly. "I'm really afraid for my life."

"This is not 1963," he said. "I don't think your neighbors are going to crucify you. The klan's not what it used to be."

"I've seen what they can do," she said.

He promised her state protection, and repeated that without her testimony there would be no case against Chambliss. Then he reminded her that, as a minister, she had an obligation to see that justice was done.

"Some of them are crazy," she said, almost whispering.

"Maybe. But I guess this is a time in your life when you just have to decide whether you're going to do something because it's right, or let them scare you away. We really need your help."

She stared at the floor, her arms folded, and said nothing. After a long wait, she nodded. "Okay," she said.

She stood up and went to the door. That was it. As he watched her leave, Eddy felt a sense of compassion and admiration for her. To agree to testify against Robert Chambliss required a degree of courage that would be hard for someone who had not lived in the Deep South in the 1960s to understand. The deep-rooted racial feelings that prevailed at that time had seemed almost impossible to speak out against; even in 1977, there was still the shadow of those feelings and that fear.

But even with Mrs. Cobb's testimony Baxley was having misgivings about the case. Much of the story they had pieced together could not be used in court, leaving little to go on but the testimony of Mrs. Cobbs and Mrs. Glenn—not a strong case. Baxley called Eddy to see if there were any additional witnesses, but Eddy had to say no.

One night in mid-September Baxley called Chris McNair, father of Denise McNair, and then a member of the Alabama legislature. Baxley said he needed to discuss the case with him.

"Chris, this is what we've got," he said. "We know who did it. But our case is not that strong. Some of our evidence is not admissible. There are five or six men out there who were involved, and one day one of them is going to get up and testify. The next attorney general may be able to get a stronger case and win it. But if we go ahead now and lose it, it'll be gone and over forever. Chris, I want you to tell me what you think."

Without hesitation, McNair replied, "I want you to go ahead. Because once you leave office, no one will ever try to do anything."

"Okay," said Baxley. "That's what I needed to know." He called Eddy in Birmingham and told him that the grand jury would be brought back so he could seek a murder indictment against Robert E. Chambliss.

On September 24, Eddy waited in the courthouse hallway, sitting alone. An hour passed, and he saw the members of the grand jury leaving the jury room. Then George Beck came out and nodded at him. Chambliss had been indicted, he said. Eddy stared at him without much emotion—an indictment meant simply that Chambliss would stand trial before a jury. There was still a lot of work to be done. Beck walked down the hall and Eddy went with him, waiting while he called Baxley in Montgomery. Then Beck put down the receiver. His voice was deadpan. "Bill wants you to go with the sheriff's people and pick Chambliss up. He might say something."

Chambliss had already been talking, even before the grand jury went into session. Gail Tarrant said he had made threatening statements about Elizabeth Cobbs— with just a single phone call, he'd bragged, he could see that her church was bombed. He had also promised to get even with those who were investigating him.

The indictment read:

> The grand jury of said county charge that, before the finding of this indictment, Robert Edward Chambliss, whose true name is to the grand jury otherwise unknown, unlawfully and with malice aforethought killed Carol Denise McNair by perpetrating an act greatly dangerous to the lives of others, and evidencing a depraved mind regardless of human life, although without any preconceived purpose to deprive any particular person of life, by, to-wit: setting off or exploding or causing to be set off or exploded, to-wit: dynamite or other explosive, to-wit: at, under, or dangerously near, to-wit: the Sixteenth Street Baptist Church in Birmingham, Jefferson County, Alabama, during to-wit: Sunday morning church worship services or other Sunday morning church activities in the said church and while the said Carol Denise McNair was within said church, and as a proximate result thereof, unlawfully killed the said Carol Denise McNair, against the peace and dignity of the State of Alabama.

Jefferson County Sheriff Mel Bailey assigned a deputy to serve Chambliss with the arrest warrant and bring him in. Eddy rode with him. Chambliss lived in the northside of Birmingham, an area of tree-lined streets and old frame houses that often showed a need for repair. Whites were moving away from the area as more and more blacks moved in; despite the fact that by then the neighborhood was almost all black, Chambliss was still living there, in a simple white frame house with a small front yard split by a short sidewalk.

The deputy parked in front. He and Eddy went to the porch and knocked. A moment later a man appeared behind the screen door.

"Yeah?" he said, and then when he saw the deputy he held the door open, as though the visit was expected. The deputy told him he had been indicted and read his Miranda warning. Chambliss nodded and stepped back to let them enter.

Chambliss wore baggy pants and a rumpled plaid shirt with the collar turned up. His hair was thinning and gray, and some of it was cocked-up in back; his eyes were watery and narrowed. "Can you give me a moment to change shirts?" he asked. Eddy had expected wild behavior, but Chambliss seemed calm. He saw Mrs. Chambliss in the adjoining room; she had appeared in the doorway briefly but flitted away. Then Chambliss came back into the living room.

"Gotta get my hair combed before I can leave," he said. Eddy and the deputy watched while he sat down in a chair; his wife came in and combed his hair. He sat like a little boy getting ready to go off to school.

But after he was settled in the deputy's car and they were pulling out from the curb, Chambliss began talking louder and louder. "This is all politics," he said. "All it is, just politics. They're just using politics to get me arrested and in this mess so they can make some hay of it. Baxley's behind it."

"Mr. Chambliss," Eddy said. "You've had your rights

read to you, have you not?" Chambliss looked at Eddy and nodded.

"You don't have to make any statement if you don't want," Eddy said, "but is there anything you might want to tell us?"

Chambliss looked at Eddy more closely. "Who are you?"

"I'm an investigator for the attorney general's office."

He shook his head. "Hell, no, I'm not talking to you. I know you told some serious things, some lies about me, and I ain't forgettin' it."

"What lies?" Eddy asked.

"Just lies. All kinds of lies." The voice was tinged with rage now. "I'm telling you I ain't gonna forget it."

"What are you going to do, Mr. Chambliss?"

He didn't answer for a moment, just stared ahead. Then he nodded. "I ain't never run from a fight," he muttered. "I ain't afraid of Baxley, or you, or nobody."

They had reached the downtown section of Birmingham now and would soon be at the county courthouse and jail. Chambliss said, "Who was the state investigator that talked with Bobby Cherry?"

"It was me," Eddy said. "Why?"

"Well, why did you tell him that I told you he carried the bomb by the church? I never told you that."

"I never said you told me that. I just told him you had said that."

He shook his head and grunted but said nothing more. They arrived at the jail, where he was fingerprinted, photographed, booked, and sent to a cell. He would remain jailed for nearly two weeks before friends and relatives posted the bond of $200,000.

21

The day after the arrest Baxley called Eddy and said to pack some things; they were going to Texas to talk to Bobby Frank Cherry again. With Chambliss indicted, Baxley hoped Cherry might feel prompted to cooperate, in light of the chance that he too might be indicted. Perhaps now he would agree to testify.

The Grand Prairie police again arranged to have Cherry at their office. He was waiting in the same conference room in which Eddy had interviewed him earlier. When Baxley and Eddy entered he nodded briefly at them. Eddy studied him for a moment; he seemed different, more stoic. The last time he had laughed a lot and talked at length, but this time he appeared testy. Baxley asked him to cooperate, to be a witness in the case against Chambliss. Cherry puffed on a cigarette and said nothing.

"Look, we know you placed that bomb there that night," Baxley said. "Chambliss and Blanton and one other man stayed in the car and drove around the block while you walked through the alley and put the bomb down, then got back into the car."

Cherry scowled. "I don't even know Chambliss."

Baxley, sitting across the table from him, looked surprised. "What are you talking about? You mean to sit there and tell me you don't know Robert Chambliss?"

"That's what I said."

"Who are you trying to kid?" Baxley pursued, his voice

rising. "We know you were in the same klavern as him, and y'all went to meetings together."

"I said I didn't know him," Cherry repeated, standing up and leaning across the table toward Baxley.

The attorney general stood up. "And you're lying, too. You know him. If you don't want to cooperate with us, we can have you indicted and put you in jail."

They were almost nose-to-nose, glaring at each other.

"Go ahead and put me in jail," Cherry said. "I don't give a damn. You ain't got a thing on me."

"We'll see about that."

"Go ahead and arrest me."

Eddy stood up then. "Sit down, Cherry," he said, putting a hand on his shoulder. Cherry eased back into the chair, still glaring at Baxley. "I never placed no bomb," he muttered.

Baxley grinned at him. "Yeah, and you don't know Chambliss, either, isn't that right? That's what you say, but you know you know him. You and him are big klan buddies, aren't you?"

Cherry shrugged. "Well, I might know him, but we ain't good friends or nothing."

Baxley threatened to have an extradition order drawn up, but Cherry never budged. The truth was, though Baxley felt certain Cherry had been involved in the bombing, there was no witness who would testify to that. Gail Tarrant wouldn't, and Mrs. Glenn could identify no one but Chambliss. Baxley and Eddy left Texas and, for the time being, closed the book on Cherry.

A few days after the indictment was handed down, Cantrell contacted Eddy at the FBI office and said he had some new information for him. "I got a call from a lady named Yvonne Young, who used to be a friend of Ross Keith's," Cantrell said. "She wants to talk to us. Says she may have some information."

"All right, let's talk to her," Eddy said.

They called Mrs. Young and arranged to meet her at a fast

food restaurant on the north side of the city, not far from where Chambliss lived. She was waiting for them at a table. She was a dark-haired woman who appeared to be in her mid-forties.

"Sergeant Cantrell says you might have some information on this case," Eddy said.

Mrs. Young said she had been with Ross Keith one day in early September 1963, about two weeks before the church was bombed. She said they had been riding a motorcycle and stopped by the Chambliss house to visit. She said Keith and Chambliss went into another room while she and Mrs. Chambliss visited in the kitchen. She said she later asked permission to use the bathroom, and Mrs. Chambliss gave her directions, pointing down a hallway. Mrs. Young said she opened the wrong door, and instead of finding a bathroom she found Keith and Chambliss standing in a room with a box of dynamite opened on the floor. "They looked like big firecrackers," she said.

Chambliss had become angry, she said, and ordered her out of the room.

"And when did you say this was?" Eddy asked.

"About two weeks before the church was bombed," she replied.

They asked her to repeat the story, asking questions from time to time. After about an hour, Eddy asked if she would testify to what she had seen that day in 1963; she said she would.

Baxley sent Eddy to the West Coast for another interview with Rowe, but it produced nothing new, even though the former FBI informant had agreed to undergo hypnosis through part of the session. He did tell Eddy of a meeting of a klan klavern called Eastview 13, during which Chambliss was accused by another member of bombing the church. Rowe said a leader named Robert Thomas had confronted Chambliss with doing the bombing, saying the deed was going to get Eastview 13 members in trouble. Chambliss had reacted angrily, Rowe said, shouting at

Thomas, "I'm tired of you trying to run everything. Go get fucked and mind your own business." Then he had paced about, shouting at other members, including Rowe, "You're all a bunch of fuckoffs, a bunch of loudmouths. You don't do shit."

In his report, Eddy later wrote, "Rowe mentioned shooting a negro and killing him on his way home during a riot in 1963. He stated he reported this to FBI and they checked it. They asked him who knew about it and he told them a Sgt. with BPD and the Sgt. had told him to go home and forget it. The FBI [McFall] told him not to talk about it. Rowe stated that the FBI would pull this from his file also."

But Birmingham Police Sergeant Earnest Cantrell had found the man shot by Rowe, and he was very much alive. "Rowe thought he killed him," he said. "But the bullet did not penetrate the brain. As near as I can tell, there had been a fight near the home of Arthur Shores the night that his home was bombed. Rowe was nearby. There was rioting that night. Anyway, a taxi cab had broken down or something right near the scene, and Rowe was there and there was a fracas, and some white people got beat up. But Rowe shot a man in the back of the head. We later found the man living in Tuscaloosa. He had lived."

There was even a report in the Birmingham police files—one that Eddy found without merit—claiming Rowe had once been seen with assassin Lee Harvey Oswald. Captain LeGrand said he had been advised that a man resembling Oswald had been seen in Birmingham with Rowe in early 1963.

Eddy interviewed a former klansman named William Jackson, whose term in the KKK had been short. But in September 1963 Jackson had attended a meeting near the Cahaba River a few miles southeast of Birmingham. The meeting had been attended by Chambliss, Blanton, and Troy Ingram, and FBI sources had said the men wanted to form their own klan group because the main organization—the United Klans of America, headed by Robert Shelton, a Tuscaloosa rubber worker—had not been "active" enough.

Jackson said he honestly did not remember much about the meeting but would testify for the state if that would help. "Would you agree to go under hypnosis if that would help you remember?" Eddy asked him.

"Yes, I would agree," he said. "I've never been hypnotized before."

Eddy contacted Dr. Hilda Tant, a Birmingham psychologist, who arranged to see Jackson that same day, October 25, 1977. Under hypnosis, Jackson gave the following story: On September 8, 1963, a week before the bombing, he was with a man named Johnny Lee, who took him to the home of Robert Chambliss to see about joining the klan. He said Chambliss told him someone would get in touch with him. On September 21, a Saturday, he said he received a call from Tommy Blanton, Jr., who told him to be at a restaurant the following day at noon. That next day Blanton met Jackson and drove him to the meeting place on the Cahaba River. Under hypnosis, Jackson recalled that there were eleven people there who signed a paper. After the meeting, he said, they went to the home of Troy Ingram.

At that point in his recollections Jackson became quite upset, said Dr. Tant. She told Eddy he became nervous and began talking rapidly. "I don't want to be here," he said repeatedly. "These are childish people. . . . They are no-good people. I want to go home. I want to go home. I don't want to be here. I want to go home."

Dr. Tant told Eddy she was convinced that Jackson had such feelings of guilt about what he heard at this meeting that he could not bear to force himself to remember. She said she felt certain Jackson had heard some conversation about the church bombing.

The Ku Klux Klan was active in Birmingham and throughout much of Alabama during the years of the civil rights movement. This rally occurred near Tuscaloosa in 1963, around the time of the church bombing. (Courtesy *The Birmingham News*)

Bob Eddy was assigned to investigate the bombing in 1976, thirteen years after the incident. Eddy's success in locating witnesses and convincing them to testify against the Ku Klux Klan led to the indictment and conviction of a klansman. (Photo by Frank Sikora)

At the time of his trial in 1977, longtime klansman Robert Chambliss was seventy-three years old. A jury found him guilty of murder for his part in the bombing. (Courtesy *The Birmingham News*)

Alabama Attorney General Bill Baxley (at left), shown here arriving at the Jefferson County Courthouse with Birmingham Police Captain Jack LeGrand, brought Chambliss to trial in late 1977, fourteen years after the bombing and seven years after Baxley had reopened the investigation. No indictments had resulted from five years of FBI investigation immediately following the crime. The jury that convicted Chambliss was the first in the deep South to find a white person guilty of murder in a race-related killing. (Courtesy *The Birmingham News*)

Elizabeth Hood Cobbs, whose testimony helped link klansman Chambliss to the church bombing, is shown here leaving the courtroom. (Courtesy *The Birmingham News*)

A statue of Martin Luther King, Jr., his face turned toward the Sixteenth Street Baptist Church, was erected in Kelly Ingram Park twenty-three years after the church bombing. The inscription on the base of the statue quotes King's description of himself as "a drum major for peace" and proclaims: "His dream liberated Birmingham from itself and began a new day of love, mutual respect, and cooperation." (Photo by Paula Dennis)

I TOLD THE PEOPLE TO
REMEMBER THE LESSON

22

On Monday, November 14, 1977, at 9:00 A.M. in Circuit Courtroom 306 at the Jefferson County Courthouse, Robert Chambliss went on trial. The courtroom was packed with spectators and news reporters.

Chambliss looked trim in a brown suit with a white shirt with tie. His whitish hair was combed to one side. His mouth was fixed in a firm line, but he grinned briefly at reporters.

Late in October one of his attorneys, Arthur Hanes, Jr., had entered a motion to quash the indictment on the grounds that fourteen years was too long a time between the alleged crime and the indictment. Hanes contended that Alabama had denied Chambliss's right to due process and a speedy trial. Jefferson County Circuit Judge Wallace Gibson, a stocky, gray-haired man, denied the motion.

After selection of the jury—nine whites, three blacks—and the usual motions, the state called its first witness, Birmingham Police Sergeant Earnest Cantrell. Cantrell testified that he had often heard citizens refer to Chambliss as "Dynamite Bob." Captain LeGrand followed, saying he had heard the nickname "Dynamite Chambliss."

The Reverend John Haywood Cross, pastor of the church at the time of the bombing, testified that he had been upstairs at the moment the explosion occurred. "It sounded like the whole world was shaking," he said, in response to questioning by John Yung. "The building, I thought, was going to collapse. And momentarily, I jerked my head. All around me was so much dust and soot—and glass had fallen, and plaster—it was so smoky in there, and some of the people could not be identified three feet from me."

"What if anything did you do after the explosion?" Yung asked.

"I asked them to vacate the building, thinking maybe something, another explosion, might go off. And then I thought about the children downstairs and I went down the stairs to the lower auditorium. I moved around frantically, checking each room."

Cross described a scene of bleeding people groping their way through smoke. He went outside then, and someone gave him a loudspeaker to talk to the crowd.

"I told the people to remember the lesson. I said the lesson for the day was love and that we should be forgiving, as Christ was forgiving—'Father, forgive them, for they know not what they do.' And then we began digging, some civil defense workers and myself. We must have gone down one or two feet and someone said, 'I feel something soft.' It was a body, and we pulled that one out and dug a little deeper, and there was a second one and a third one and finally a fourth one. They were all found on top of one another."

"Reverend, did you know the individuals whose bodies you found on top of each other?" Yung asked.

"Yes."

"Who were they?"

"Annie Mae Collins [actually Addie Mae], Cynthia Wesley, Carole Robertson, and Denise McNair."

Cross said they heard moans coming from nearby, and they kept digging till they found Addie's younger sister, Sarah Collins.

By the time of the trial, Sarah Collins Riley was twenty-seven years old. Questioned by Yung, she recalled the moment the bomb went off. Defense Attorney Arthur Hanes,

Jr., objected to the word "bomb," and from then on in the trial it was not used. To clarify the point, Judge Gibson asked Mrs. Riley, "Was there an explosion?"

"Yes, there was," she said.

"Do you recall exactly what you were doing?" Yung asked.

"I was in the ladies' lounge with the other four girls. I was at the washbowl at the time."

Yung nodded. "And do you remember where the other four girls, who have been named, including your sister, were at the time?"

She gestured with a hand. "Yes. They were over by the window."

"Did you see your sister immediately prior to the explosion?" Yung asked.

"Yes. My sister was tying Denise McNair's sash on her dress."

"Is that the last time you saw your sister?"

"Yes."

"Have you seen Cynthia Wesley or Carole Robertson since that time?"

"No."

"Tell the jury what you remember happened after the explosion."

Mrs. Riley glanced briefly at the jury, then back to Yung. "Right after the explosion, I called my sister."

"What did you say?"

"I said—I called about three times—I said, 'Addie! Addie! Addie!'"

Yung paused. Mrs. Riley's words hung over the courtroom. Finally he asked, "Did Addie answer you?"

"No, she didn't."

"What happened after that?"

"Then I heard somebody calling out," she said. "They said that somebody had bombed the church."

Hanes objected to the word "bomb," but Judge Gibson overruled, saying she was testifying to what she heard somebody say.

Mrs. Riley continued, "Then somebody came and brought me outside."

"Were you taken to a hospital?"

"Yes."

"Could you see?"

"No."

"How long was it before you could see?"

"About a month."

"Out of both eyes?"

"No, just the left."

"Do you still have your right eye?"

"No. They had to take it out."

Dr. Joe Donald testified that he was on duty at the hospital the morning of the church bombing and saw the girls when they were brought in.

"Did you see the bodies as depicted in this picture?" asked George Beck, who was handling this phase of the questioning. Beck showed him photographs of each of the girls.

Donald nodded. "I remember four colored girls that were dead."

"Describe the injuries on the body of Denise McNair."

"Abrasive and detonating type injuries," Donald replied. "The tissues were lacerated."

"Was that the cause of death?"

"Well, yes."

"When you first the saw the body of Denise McNair, was the alive, or dead?"

"She was dead."

Court adjourned till nine o'clock the next morning, when J. O. Butler took the stand. Butler had been the coroner in 1963. He testified that on the morning of the bombing he had been called to the hospital at 10:45.

"How were the bodies identified?" Beck asked.

"By their relatives," Butler answered. "And there were one or two pastors there."

"Do you know who identified the body of Denise Mc-Nair?"

"Both the father and mother," said Butler.

"Could you describe the wounds to the body of Denise McNair?"

Butler nodded, "The main injury, sir, was a fracture of the skull. There was a two-and-a-half-inch by one-and-a-half-inch fracture of the skull, and also, lacerations on the right shoulder and several more abrasions and lacerations on the side of the face."

Butler had consulted his notes for the reply and also described the wounds of the other girls. All had numerous lacerations and abrasions to the upper body. Cynthia Wesley had sustained the most pronounced impact from the detonation, he said.

"Who identified Cynthia Wesley's body?" Beck asked.

"Well, just—she was identified from her rings and clothes, sir," Butler replied.

"Any reasons for that?" Beck pursued.

"Yes, sir," the former coroner said. "The upper part of the body was badly mutilated and it was hardly recognizable."

Beck asked Butler if, as coroner, he had had occasion in the past to see the bodies of persons killed by explosion, such as at mines or construction sites. Butler said he had.

"In your best judgment, was this calculated to cause death?"

"Yes, sir."

Chris McNair was called to the stand to tell of the last day he had seen his daughter Denise alive. Beck asked him about that morning, and McNair replied that Denise, his only child, was getting ready for church. McNair's wife, Maxine, and Denise belonged to the Sixteenth Street Baptist Church, but he was a member of St. Paul Lutheran. On that morning, he said, he was ready to leave and Denise had asked him if she was riding with him, or was her mother going to drive. "We talked, and she wanted to know why couldn't I wait until she got ready," he said. "And I said I had to go and start Sunday school. I was a Sunday school superintendent, and so after I explained it to her, she said, 'Okay, Daddy, go ahead.'"

There was a long pause. Beck asked, "And did you ever see your daughter alive again?"

McNair shook his head. "No sir, I did not."

That ended Beck's questioning. At Chambliss's table, Hanes shook his head. "We have no questions, Mr. McNair."

Several days earlier, Baxley had been told by Eddy that Civil Defense Captain James Lay—the witness who had told the FBI in 1963 about two white men near the church during the early morning hours of September 2—had refused to testify. "Tall Paul" White, the radio disk jockey who also saw two men there that night, had agreed to take the stand, but Baxley needed Lay, a strong witness who had identified one of the men as looking like Chambliss and the other as resembling Tommy Blanton, Jr. Because White could not identify the men he'd seen, his testimony could support Lay's account but would not be helpful if Lay refused to take the stand.

Baxley went to see Lay several times. Each time Lay said that he couldn't remember or that he suffered from amnesia. He would complain that he was not listened to in 1963 so he was not going to get involved now. "But I'm listening to you now," Baxley implored. "I'm doing something now. I've been working on this thing for six years. But I need your help. You can help us get the ones responsible for killing those little girls."

But Lay did not budge.

On the Sunday morning before the trial was to begin, Baxley called Chris McNair and asked him to invite Lay over for breakfast. He was convinced that once Lay sat at the same breakfast table with the father of one of the girls killed in the bombing he would agree to take the stand. Mc-

Nair fixed eggs, bacon, and toast, and Lay was there when Baxley arrived. Lay ate bacon and eggs with them, listened to both of them make appeals for his testimony, then told them he could not remember well and had amnesia. He added that if he testified and missed work, he would surely be fired.

Later, an angry Baxley told his staff to subpoena Lay for trial, which would not force him to testify but would require his presence at the courthouse. "If he won't help us," he said, "then we'll keep the son-of-a-bitch tied down at the courthouse while the trial goes on. He'll have to come there every day." Under these conditions, there was a slim chance Lay might change his mind and agree to testify.

But meanwhile, Tall Paul White had not shown up at the courthouse as Baxley had expected, and so Eddy was sent out to find him. Eddy and other investigators made a futile search of the city. White was not at home, not at the radio station where he worked, not at any of the places he was known to frequent. Baxley was furious. "There are two black men who could help with this," he said. "And neither one of them will do it."

23

On Wednesday, November 16, 1977, Baxley called Eddy shortly after six A.M. "Bob, we're going to use Mrs. Cobbs today," he said, "so get her over there and have her ready."

"Okay." Eddy glanced at his watch. "What time you think you'll put her on?"

"Well, have her there this morning, but it may not be until this afternoon," Baxley said.

Eddy called Elizabeth Cobbs. She answered the phone after just one ring, as though she had been expecting a call.

"Elizabeth? Bob."

"I know," she said. "Is this the day?"

"This is the day." There was a pause. "Are you ready?"

She didn't answer for a while. Finally, she said, "I guess so."

He drove to her apartment. Her face was pale and drawn. "Now, don't be worried," he told her. "This'll be over before long."

"I'll be glad when it is." Her words were flat, somber. She wore a necklace with a large crucifix. She said she was frightened by the thought of Chambliss being in the same room with her.

"He'll be there," Eddy said. "Sure. But don't let that worry you. Just don't look at him. Just look at the attorney who is asking you questions and answer them as best you can. Keep your eyes on the attorney."

"Don't look at anyone else?" she asked.

"Well, if the judge should ask you anything you can look at him," he said. "But other than that, just look at me if you want. But don't look at Chambliss."

When they got to the courthouse he took her to a second-floor room—little more than a closet, actually, though it did contain a table and chair. She was to remain there, out of sight of other witnesses and anyone else. "Just sit here and take it easy," he told her. "I'll come and get you when it's time."

She looked around the cramped quarters and nodded. He went upstairs to the courtroom. From time to time, he went back down to make sure she was all right. He didn't doubt for a minute that klansmen might try to kill her if they thought they had a chance. But except for him and Jefferson County District Attorney Earl Morgan and his deputy David Barber, no one knew where she was.

Early in the afternoon Baxley signalled to Eddy, who hurried down the stairs and opened the door to the room. "Elizabeth?"

She started crying then, but stood up and came into the hall. Eddy couldn't think of anything to say except, "It's going to be all right. Don't worry. It's all going to be all right."

They walked down the hallway to the courtroom. Her crying worried him. "You okay now?" he muttered.

She wiped at her eyes and nodded, and he opened the courtroom door.

A sheriff's deputy blocked the entrance. "You can't come in" he whispered loudly. "Judge says no one can come or go."

"You're kidding! This is the witness they're waiting for."

The deputy shook his head. "You can't come in."

"I'm with Baxley's office," Eddy said. But the deputy closed the door. This was absurd. Eddy looked at Mrs. Cobbs in disbelief. She looked back at him but saw nothing funny about it. It just added to the agony of waiting, heightening the dread she must have felt. They sat down on a wooden bench in the hallway. Later he would learn that when Baxley called for Mrs. Cobbs he asked the judge to seal the courtroom for security reasons, to allow no one in or out. The deputy had taken the order at face value. So Eddy and the witness waited outside the courtroom until the attorneys and the judge began to grow impatient. Finally the door opened and the somewhat bewildered deputy looked out at them and asked in a stage whisper, "Is that Mrs. Cobbs?"

"You got it," Eddy said.

"They're waiting on you," the deputy said. Then, he shook his head. "I'm sorry. I didn't know that was you. They said to not let anybody in."

"I understand," Eddy said. He led Elizabeth into the courtroom, aware of the hush in the place, aware of the heads turning and the eyes fixed on them. Everyone was watching her. But she was walking with more resolve, and when she got to the witness stand, he saw her eyes open wider till she stared directly at the bailiff as he administered the oath.

Eddy took a seat near the end of the first row on the right side. He sat sideways, so he could keep his eyes both on her and on Chambliss and the crowd. He didn't want anyone making any gestures or facial movements that would intimidate her. She stated her name and said she was pastor of Denman Memorial Methodist Church.

"Mrs. Cobbs, I will ask you whether or not you are in any way related to this defendant, Robert E. "Bob" Chambliss," John Yung said.

"He is married to my mother's sister," she replied.

"Do you recall on September 15, 1963, the bombing of the—"

"Objection," said Hanes.

Yung continued. "The *explosion* at the Sixteenth Street Baptist Church here in Birmingham?"

"Yes, sir, I do." She gazed squarely into Yung's eyes.

"In which four young girls were killed?"

"Yes, sir."

Yung asked if she had seen Chambliss the day before the explosion, and she replied that she had gone to his house to visit Mrs. Chambliss, who had been ill. The visit had been on the Saturday morning before the bombing. Chambliss, she said, was in an "agitated" mood, because the newspaper carried a story that a young white girl had been cut on the arm by a black youth, in an incident apparently related to the turmoil surrounding school desegregation. Chambliss, she said, had used vile language.

At that point Judge Gibson interrupted. "I'm not trying to embarrass the witness, but I think the language . . . I mean, sometimes we can't deal in niceties and I think this is one of those times."

"All right, Mrs. Cobbs," said Yung. "What the judge is saying is that he needs to hear your testimony as to what he said when he became angry . . . and started saying things against, or about, blacks."

She nodded. "He said that if anyone had backed him up, that they would have had the g.d. niggers in their place by now. He always used the term 'nigger' when referring to blacks."

"Did he often use profanity?"

"Often."

"Did he say 'g.d.'?"

"No."

"Did he say what the words 'g.d.' stand for?"

"Yes, sir."

"Can you describe his demeanor, or his tone of voice?"

"He was very agitated, very angry. He said he had been fighting a one-man war."

"What else did he say?" Yung asked.

"He said George Wallace was a coward, or he could have stopped all this."

Later, she said, Chambliss asked his wife to comb his hair, then left the house, returning after a short time with a newspaper. Then he sat down at the kitchen table reading the story about the cutting incident.

"He started again," she said, "very loudly and angrily, cursing, swearing. He said if he had been there that that nigger wouldn't have gotten away."

"Those were his words?" Yung asked.

"Yes, sir."

"What else was said?"

"He said that he had gotten the address of the, quote, nigger girl that was going to integrate the school. I cautioned him against doing anything foolish and he said, 'Don't worry,' that if he did anything, it would be something he could get away in."

"Something that he could get away in?"

"Yes, sir."

"He said that on the morning of the 14th?"

"Yes, sir," Mrs. Cobbs answered firmly.

"Was anything else said that you recall?" Yung pursued.

"He told me that he had enough stuff put away to flatten half of Birmingham."

Yung stared at her, then gestured toward Chambliss. "This defendant, Robert Chambliss—"

"Yes, sir," she said, nodding.

"—said that he had enough stuff put away to flatten half of Birmingham?"

"Say it one more time," snapped Hanes.

"Yes, sir," she said, still looking at Yung.

"And this was the day before the explosion at the Sixteenth Street Baptist Church?" Yung asked.

"Yes, sir."

"Did he say anything else, Mrs. Cobbs?"

She fingered the cross hanging down from her neck. "He told me that the FBI or police could pick him up and search all they wanted to but they wouldn't find it unless he pointed it out to them."

"Find what?" asked Yung.

"The stuff," she replied.

"Is that his words?"

"Yes, sir."

"The stuff that would flatten half of Birmingham?"

She nodded. "Yes, sir."

"Did you make any reply or say anything after he made that statement?"

She paused while she considered the question. Then she said, "I asked him what good he thought any of that would do."

"Did he say anything?" Yung asked.

"At that point he placed his hand upon the newspaper in front of him," she said. "He looked me in the face and said, 'You just wait until after Sunday morning. And they will beg us to let them segregate.'"

Yung, with his arms folded, slowly repeated the words attributed to Chambliss. "You just wait until after Sunday morning and they will beg us to let them segregate?"

"Yes, sir."

"On Sunday morning, September the fifteenth, is that correct?" he asked.

"Yes, sir."

Yung nodded. "Mrs. Cobbs, what if anything else was said?"

"I asked him what he meant, and all he would say was, 'Just wait. You'll see.'"

"Just wait," Yung repeated. "You will see?"

"Yes."

Then Yung asked, "*Did* you see?"

Hanes interrupted, "Judge, wait. Just a minute. I move to exclude that."

"Sustained," said the judge, nodding.

Hanes continued. "I ask for a mistrial on that point, Judge."

"Ladies and gentlemen," Judge Gibson said, looking at the jury, "don't consider that question or that answer."

After some further legal debate, Yung continued his questioning. "Did the defendant make any further statements after the explosion at the church?"

"Yes, he did," she said. "To the best of my recollection, it was the following Saturday evening. He was seated on the sofa in the living room. He was watching television. A news broadcast came on concerning the investigation of the church explosion."

"Did he make a statement during that news broadcast?" Yung asked.

She nodded. "The announcer said there was the possibility of murder charges being made."

"What, if anything, did he say?"

"He said it wasn't meant to hurt anybody. It didn't go off when it was supposed to."

"To whom did he make that statement, Mrs. Cobbs?" Yung asked.

She lifted her hands in a questioning gesture. "To the television announcer, I assume."

"Did he say anything to you?"

"No."

"Did you say anything to him?"

"No, sir."

Yung consulted his notes briefly, then asked, "What else—had he made any other statement prior to the explosion?"

She said there had been other statements that arose when he heard of events surrounding the desegregation of Birmingham schools. "He said he was helping stop integration in the schools."

"Did he say anything else?"

"He spoke of being present at demonstrations," she said.

Yung asked, "Did he say what he was attempting to do?"

"To preserve white supremacy, and keep the niggers in their place," she said.

"Did he say whether or not he was in, or part of, any organization in this connection?"

"He was a member of the Ku Klux Klan," she said.

"Did he tell you why he was a member of, or what the Ku Klux Klan was planning to do?"

"In order to fight to maintain segregation and keep the niggers in their place," she replied.

"Did he state to you how that was to be done by him through the Ku Klux Klan?" Yung asked.

Elizabeth kept her eyes on Yung. "Many times he said that he would do anything possible."

"Anything possible?"

"Yes, sir."

"That's all."

Hanes stood up and approached the witness stand.

"You have heard George Wallace say that he was fighting to help save segregation, haven't you?"

"Yes, sir," she said.

"And you have heard many people in Jefferson County say that, have you not?"

"Yes, sir."

"And at that time, your uncle was—what—sixty years old?" Hanes asked.

"Approximately."

"You were talking about 'stuff.' Did you ever see any 'stuff,' please, ma'am?"

"That is his words, Mr. Hanes," she replied.

"I am asking you, did you ever see any?" Hanes pressed.

"That's a question I cannot answer, Mr. Hanes, unless you define what you're asking me."

"Ma'am?"

"You asked me what he said?" She had a puzzled look on her face.

Hanes shrugged. "So you don't even know what 'stuff' is, is that correct?"

"He did not tell me."

"How old are—I hate to ask you how old you are now, please, ma'am?"

"I am thirty-seven," she said.

"That would have made you twenty-three then, is that correct? Did you make any notes on alleged conversations at the time they were had?"

She shook her head. "Mental notes only, sir."

"Oh, I see. Did you write down any of these things?"

"No, sir."

Hanes questioned her about how many times she had told her account, or was this the first time she was reporting it.

She replied that she had first told lawmen about it shortly after the bombing.

"When did you become a preacher?" Hanes asked.

"About two years ago."

He paused. "Was that before or after you divorced your previous husband?"

"After," she replied quickly.

Baxley stood up, "We object. That has no bearing at all."

Judge Gibson nodded. "Yes. I sustain the objection. I don't know what possible probative value it would have on the issues involved in this case."

Hanes flipped through his notes. Then he asked, "Did you apply for any reward in 1963?"

"No, sir."

"Mrs. Cobbs, you testified to some hard words. Are you positive that your sixty-year old uncle, in Birmingham, Alabama, in 1963, used the word 'nigger'? Are you sure of that?"

"I'm certain," she said.

"Ever heard anyone else talk rough like that, Mrs. Cobbs?"

She shook her head. "Not exactly, no."

"I don't have any further questions," Hanes said, then suddenly raised a hand to nullify the statement. "You didn't know what he was talking about when he said, 'Wait until Sunday,' did you?"

"At the time I wasn't sure," she answered. "I was frightened by the remark."

Hanes sat down then and gestured toward Yung, who rose for the redirect phase of the questioning.

"Did you ever hear George Wallace, or anybody else, state that they had enough 'stuff' to flatten half of Birmingham?" he asked.

"No, sir."

"That's all," Yung said.

When Hanes questioned her again as to how well she could remember things Chambliss had said, she told him that she recalled the events vividly.

"It was a weekend I'll never forget," she said.

24

———
———
———

Elizabeth Cobbs, who had been on the stand for more than two hours, walked out of the courtroom quickly. Eddy followed her down the aisle. Out in the hall she shook her head several times. "Can we leave?" she asked, her voice urgent.

He walked her out of the building, and they went to the restaurant at the Holiday Inn. He figured she would be famished, but she was not hungry. She only wanted coffee. He sat with her for thirty minutes or so, watching her smoke one cigarette after another. She had done fine, he told her. Remarkably well. Her testimony had been the most damaging aspect of the case against Chambliss. Later, an FBI agent drove her to her apartment, and Eddy returned to the courtroom.

That afternoon several FBI agents joined him in trying to find another witness, a woman who had been klansman Ross Keith's girlfriend in the 1960s. Yvonne Fike Young had agreed to testify but had failed to show up at the courthouse. They found her at home, and when she came to the door she appeared hostile.

"What is it now?" she asked.

"Mrs. Young," Eddy said, "we were looking for you at the courthouse today."

"I don't want to testify," she said.

"But you said you would," he said. "You told Bill Baxley you would."

"I don't want to get involved in it," she said. "Please leave."

"Well, we'll leave," he said, "but I'll be back with a court order. You can have it your way."

"I don't know that much," she protested. "Why do I have to?"

"Just come on down and tell what you do know," he said. "There's nothing to be afraid of. There've been two dozen witnesses down there so far and nobody's been hurt. You'll be safe."

She stood with her arms folded, gazing beyond him, out into space. At last, apparently feeling they would bring her into court one way or another, Mrs. Young said she would come down to the courthouse. She started to get her coat and come right then, but he told her she could wait until the next morning. She nodded.

The next day Yvonne Fike Young appeared as promised. As she prepared to testify, Eddy saw Chambliss looking at her with a perplexed expression on his face.

Under questioning by Beck, she said she and Ross Keith had gone to the Chamblisses' home two weeks before the bombing, and while the men had talked she had visited with Mrs. Chambliss in the kitchen. Then, she said, she had asked to use the restroom. Mrs. Chambliss gave her directions and she said she walked down a hallway. "I started to the restroom, and I went to the wrong door," she said.

"You say you went to the wrong door?" Beck asked.

"Yes, sir."

"Who told you that it was the wrong door?"

"Ross," she replied. "Ross Keith."

"Did you open that door?"

"Yes, sir."

"What did you do? What happened when you opened the door?"

"When I opened the door, and at that particular time Mr. Chambliss started cussing. He scolded me as though I was a child, that I had done something real bad. He told Ross that the door was supposed to have been locked, and he knew not to carry me to that door."

"Did Mr. Chambliss appear to be angry?"

"Yes, and he was cussing," Mrs. Young said.

"Did you open the door?" Beck asked.

"I had already opened the door," she said. "I cannot remember any furniture, and there were things on the floor."

"What did you see there on the floor?"

"When I opened the door there were three or four bundles lying on the floor," she said. "There were four or five articles to the bundles. They were tied with a cord like you would fix a package to mail with."

"Well, now, could you be more specific about the bundles?" Beck asked. "What did they look like?"

She replied quickly. "They looked like oversize firecrackers."

"Can you tell us what color they were?"

"They were between a beige and a brown."

"And can you describe how Mr. Chambliss appeared after that?"

"He was still mad when we left," she said.

Hanes, upon cross-examination, questioned her about her ability to recall events fourteen years after they had occurred and asked why she hadn't said anything earlier. She replied that she had told the FBI in 1963.

"Let me ask you this: Did you not receive shock treatments at the psychiatric unit at University Hospital?"

"Yes, I did. It was at my request."

Later he asked, "Have you filed for any reward, or did you know of a reward?"

"I read about it in the newspaper," she said. "But that's blood money and I want no part of it."

At another point he asked if she had known that in 1963 Bobby Kennedy had been in charge of the Justice Department and the FBI. Baxley objected, and Judge Gibson noted, "I don't see that Bobby Kennedy has anything to do with it."

"Well, he does, Your Honor," Hanes said. "Because, well,

149

if Bill Baxley is prosecuting, then Bobby Kennedy is prosecuting." (Hanes later said that the evidence on which Baxley based his prosecution in 1977 was the same as the evidence on which Kennedy had decided not to prosecute in 1963.)

Gertrude Glenn, the witness who had been visiting from Detroit at the time of the bombing, took the stand and stuck to her original account: she had seen several white men sitting in a car near the Sixteenth Street Baptist Church at 2:00 A.M. on September 15, just eight hours before the explosion occurred. She said the dome light was on inside the car and she recognized a man who looked like Chambliss. Her time on the stand was marked by numerous legal hassles and objections. As Eddy listened to bits of it, he couldn't help but think how much more powerful the case would have been had he been able to get Gail Tarrant to testify.

FBI agent John McCormick testified that he had been through training in explosions in bombings and had been around many dynamite explosions. He said that the odor that remains following a dynamite explosion gave him a headache. On the afternoon of September 15, he said, he was sent to the bombed church to assist in the investigation and developed a "bad" headache. He also said he was present when agents found a small fishing bobber with a wire attached to it. The wire, he said, was not fishing line but made of a sturdier material. Under cross-examination, he testified that he did not know what had become of the fishing bobber, that he had not personally sent it to the FBI laboratory. (The bobber seems to have disappeared— records showed it was sent to the lab, but there is nothing to indicate it ever arrived there in the weeks following the bombing.)

Earnest Cantrell was called to the witness stand a second time and recounted under questioning by Baxley that in November of 1976—when word was out that Baxley was reopening the investigation into the church bombing— Chambliss had come to the Birmingham Police Department to talk to officers about a former klansman, Don Luna, who had been arrested on a securities violation. It was Luna who in 1963 had given state agents information that Chambliss had purchased some dynamite; Chambliss had been arrested and fined, and apparently he wanted to get back at Luna if he could. "He did about eighty-five percent of the talking," Cantrell said. Chambliss told Cantrell and other officers in the room that on September 4, 1963, he had gone to a store owned by klansman Leon Negron and purchased either a case or a partial case of dynamite. Cantrell recounted that Chambliss said Negron had told him, "If you're going to blow up some niggers, I will throw in a few extra sticks." Cantrell also quoted Chambliss as saying, "They thought I bombed the church. If I had bombed the church, I would have put enough stuff there to flatten the damn thing."

Then Cantrell said the conversation took a startling turn. "Mr. Chambliss stated to me that—I quote—'A fellow told me how to make a bomb by using a drip method.' He said, 'You would use a bucket of water and a fishing bobber, with a hole in the bottom of the bucket.'"

"Chambliss told you that?" Baxley answered.

"Yes, sir."

"Did you or anybody in your presence ask Chambliss anything at that time?"

Cantrell nodded. "Captain LeGrand asked him who told him this. He said he didn't remember."

Birmingham fire marshal Aaron Rosenfeld testified that he heard the sound of the explosion that morning and later went to the scene. He said he noticed a hole in the wall of the church and saw a crater dug in the ground leading away from the blasted window. He said he went to the furrow in the ground and reached into it.

"When you reached into that crater, what did you do, if anything?" asked Yung.

"Well, I got some dirt from underneath it and smelled it."

"Smelled it?"

"Yes, sir."

"Did you recognize that smell?"

"Yes, sir."

"What was that smell?"

"Dynamite."

William E. Berry, who was the assistant fire marshal, testified that he, too, smelled dynamite when he arrived at the church. He also stated that, based on his training, experience, and investigation, the explosion at the church was not a natural gas explosion; had it been, fire would have flashed through the area and blown out the structure at its weakest point, which would have been at the perimeter or outer edges of the building, he said. At the bombed church, Berry found that the explosion had the most destructive force concentrated at its center, which was the crater; the destructive force of the explosion had diminished as it went out. He further stated that he determined that the explosion was caused by a high explosive such as dynamite—the noise of the blast was consistent with a dynamite explosion.

The state rested, and Hanes presented the defense's case, calling several character witnesses, all of whom said that Chambliss was a fine man with a good reputation. None had heard anything bad about him. Baxley asked each of them: "Did you know this man was arrested for beating a black? And that when the beating had occurred, he had been wearing a Ku Klux Klan mask?" No, none of them knew that.

"Did you know he had bragged that he had done some of the bombings in Birmingham?" Again, none had ever heard that. They had all heard only good things.

After the final character witness said she had not heard any bad things about Chambliss, Baxley reversed his questioning: "Have you—can you give me the names of any persons who have had anything good to say about Robert Chambliss?"

After a long pause, she said she couldn't.

25

Arthur Hanes, Jr., had been involved in big cases before. He had been retained to defend James Earl Ray, accused assassin of Dr. Martin Luther King, Jr., and had assisted his father in defending three klansmen charged with the night-rider slaying of Viola Liuzzo following the Selma-to-Montgomery march in 1965. The three had been acquitted on murder charges but were found guilty on a federal charge of violating the victim's civil rights. Hanes and his father, Arthur Hanes, Sr., a former FBI agent and former mayor of Birmingham, had worked as a team, but in the Chambliss case the elder Hanes had turned over most of the work to his son.

From the moment the trial started, there had been speculation that Chambliss would take the stand and declare his innocence; in later years, Hanes, Jr., would recall that he had advised his client that such a course was the only chance of getting an acquittal. But as Hanes stood at the defense table and prepared to announce his chief witness, Robert Chambliss, he noticed that the defendant was not making any moves to go to the witness stand. In a hushed tone Hanes said, "Robert, get up and go to the witness stand."

Chambliss didn't budge. He sat staring straight ahead.

"Robert, get up there."

"I ain't goin'," Chambliss shot back in a stage whisper. "No, sir, I ain't goin'."

Hanes sat down and leaned over toward him. "You gotta be kidding. Get up there, Robert. You have to take the stand."

"No, sir," Chambliss repeated, shaking his head.

Judge Gibson suggested a recess. As the jury left the courtroom, Hanes hurried Chambliss to a conference room and repeatedly asked him to testify, stressing that if he did not he stood a good chance of being convicted. He refused. "Okay, Robert," the attorney finally conceded. "But I'm not the one who'll be going to jail."

On Thursday morning, November 17, Hanes rested his defense, and closing arguments began. Assistant Attorney General George Beck stood before the jury and read the indictment, then summarized the evidence presented. "It is your duty to convict Robert Chambliss of first-degree murder," he said.

Hanes tried to refute the evidence, saying Chambliss was at home playing dominoes when the bomb went off. As for Elizabeth Cobbs, he said, the words she heard from Chambliss were "just his talk"; in 1963 many white Alabamians were talking about stopping integration. Yvonne Fike Young, he said, was an unreliable witness who had hallucinations. "It takes a lot of courage to stick to the evidence," Hanes said, "and not be swayed by some external, emotional thing."

He paused, and then told the jury, "If you render a verdict of not guilty you can say to your friends, 'I didn't avenge anything. I didn't change anything. But I wasn't sworn to do that.'"

When Baxley came forward to conclude the state's presentation, he held pictures of the four girls in his hand. "Today," he said, "is Denise McNair's birthday."

The words hung over the courtroom.

"And if she had lived," he went on, "she would have been twenty-six."

He went over the evidence again, telling how a bomb placed at the church had snuffed out the lives of four children, four girls. He gestured toward Chambliss.

"If you feel sympathy for him because of his age," he said, "look at these pictures." He placed the coroner's photos of the girls in front of the jurors—pictures showing Denise McNair's lifeless eyes, Cynthia Wesley's mutilated upper body.

"When that blast went off," Baxley said, "it was truly a bomb heard round the world. The crime was against all of us, against the people of Birmingham and the state of Alabama.

"Give Denise McNair a birthday present."

The jury deliberated for several hours that day and then resumed early the next morning. Baxley did not wait. He left the courthouse after his closing argument, stopped for a sandwich, and told an assistant he wanted to take a walk. He didn't say where he was going, but he had told himself that he had to go to the church. He walked the five blocks and slowly ascended the front steps but found the door locked. He tried another door, which opened, and walked inside. The sanctuary was empty, though he could hear voices coming from the basement, possibly from some kind of meeting.

Baxley stood for a moment, then walked slowly to the front of the sanctuary, stopping at the plaque with the pictures of Denise, Carole, Addie Mae, and Cynthia. He stood gazing at them. Then, closing his eyes, he spoke an improvised prayer: "Lord, thank you for letting me live long enough to do this."

As he finished, he looked again at the plaque.

Suddenly, he heard a sound, and a voice asked, "What are you doing here?" Baxley turned and saw a man, apparently a church member, standing about ten feet away, staring suspiciously at him.

"I was just looking at these pictures," he told the man.

"Well, you gotta leave."

Baxley nodded. "Okay."

The man, who had not recognized him, stood watching until the attorney general left the church.

On Friday morning, November 18, 1977, the jury reported to the judge that it had reached a verdict. Beck, Yung, and Eddy hurried to the packed courtroom. Chambliss, his face tense, was blinking rapidly as he watched the jury. Then his eyes dropped to the floor.

The words seemed to echo across the courtroom. "We, the jury, find the defendant, Robert Edward Chambliss, guilty of murder."

Chambliss stared at the jury foreman. His eyes narrowed, and he wavered slightly as he stood. The jury recommended life in prison, and Judge Gibson asked Chambliss if he had anything to say before sentence was pronounced.

Chambliss nodded. "Judge, I swear to God I didn't bomb that church," he said, his voice hoarse but high-pitched. "I never bombed nothing. I never hurt nobody. I have never been near that church."

Gibson gazed at him. "The sentence is life in prison. The defendant is remanded to the custody of the sheriff."

They took him away then.

Baxley, who had awaited the verdict with his wife in their motel room, later joined some of his assistants at a pub for a couple of beers. While there was some jubilation, most of the talk was subdued. Chief investigator Shows, who had been the first member of Baxley's bombing probe team, noticed that the attorney general had tears in his eyes. Shows said to himself that his boss was thinking about the four girls.

At the courthouse it struck Eddy that this had finally ended, at least his part of it, after ten months of living in the Holiday Inn. "I gotta check out of the motel," he said, but just then George Beck elbowed his way through the spectators and called to him: "Eddy, we want you to go pick up Blanton."

Eddy blinked and stared in disbelief. "Blanton? Pick him up? Why?"

"Bill said he wants you to get him and see if he'll talk," Beck said.

The last thing Eddy wanted to do just then was interview a klansman or anybody else. He was tired and wanted to go home. He had been awake almost continually for several days and nights. "George, right now my mind is just fuzzy, and if I did get Blanton to talk I don't know if I could do a good job of hearing everything he might tell me," he said.

Beck said he sympathized. But Baxley's theory was that the conviction of Chambliss might scare some of his former klan comrades to confess in return for a lighter sentence. Eddy protested further, without success. Finally, he went to a telephone and called Sergeant Cantrell, who knew where Blanton lived; he agreed to drive over with Eddy and pick him up.

Blanton, who was then in his late thirties, agreed to talk but said he wanted his attorney present. While they waited for the attorney to arrive, Eddy tried to put him at ease, making small talk. Blanton glanced at Eddy but did not answer. He simply folded his arms and stared straight ahead.

They sat in silence for about twenty minutes until attorney Louis Wilkinson arrived. Blanton was asked if he would turn state's evidence in return for a reduced sentence. "Let me talk with him," Wilkinson said, and he and Blanton left the room for twenty minutes. When they returned, Wilkinson said, "He says he doesn't know anything." That ended it. Eddy checked out of the Holiday Inn.

26

——
——
——

In 1978 Bill Baxley ran for governor of Alabama and lost. He confided to friends that the prosecution of Chambliss for the church bombing probably made the difference; while many white Alabamians applauded his effort, many others did not. His wife, Lucy, said comments were made to her when she had campaigned for him. Most of the derisive remarks were made by white men.

When Baxley's term as attorney general ended in January 1979, Bob Eddy knew his days as a special investigator were numbered. The new attorney general, Charles Graddick, did not share Baxley's enthusiasm for continuing to look into the case. Eddy stayed on and worked with John Yung to prepare for the trial of J. B. Stoner, the lawyer from Marietta, Georgia, who was leader of the National States Rights Party. Stoner and his car had been seen often before and after bombings during the civil rights era.

Evidence uncovered in the Chambliss investigation had provided information about Stoner, and he was indicted on a charge that he set an explosive device at the Bethel Baptist Church in 1958. A short time before Stoner was to go on trial in May 1980, Attorney General Graddick fired Eddy. Yung went on as chief prosecutor and won a conviction; Stoner was sentenced to ten years in prison.

Immediately after the verdict Yung called a press conference in front of the Jefferson County Courthouse in Birmingham and announced he was resigning from Graddick's staff, blasting the new attorney general for firing Eddy. Then he drove to Montgomery, where he later showed up at a party that was also attended by Bill and Lucy Baxley. The unflappable, always proper Yung spotted his former boss and went over to him. To the surprise of all, he threw his arms around him and hugged him.

"Baxley, you old S.O.B.," he said. "I love you."

In the months after his conviction, Chambliss wrote several letters claiming he had been framed and had information about who did the bombing. Eddy made several trips to the prison to see Chambliss. He looked in bad shape, his eyes sunken, his face pale and puffy. His hair had been cut short. He would pace around the cell, talking at length, but Eddy thought that what he said was incoherent.

In one of his letters, addressed to the U.S. District Court in Birmingham and dated December 1, 1981, Chambliss said,

> My appeals came up 5 times in a little over 3 months in the state of Alabama courts but my attorney Art Hanes, Sr., refused to come get me to carry me to hear my appeals. The same good white guard would bring me U.S. army brogan shoes and a new suit of prison blues and say here Chambliss get off your slides and your pajamas your attorney Art Hanes, Sr. is on his way after you now to carry you to hear your appeal. He would come back that afternoon and say Chambliss I am sorry your attorney never did get here something must have happened 5 times in a little over 3 months. I turned on my A.M. and F.M. radio one morning to hear the early morning news. The first thing came on said the Federal Judge Frank M. Johnston Jr. in New Orleans refused to hear R. E. Chambliss's appeal. I sat down right then and wrote him and said Your honor I never would have believed you would have treated me in any such way after I wrote you and told you I will knell on my mother's grave and pray to you I have

never bombed anything, killed anyone nor been in Tommie Blanton's car in my life so help me God. He investigated back in 1963 just to see who all was implicated in all the bombings never once thinking they would implicate me in 1977 and me innocent before they picked me up I was security guard for Winn Dixies in north Birmingham. There was 5 C.I.A. agents involved name Billy Holt his sorry wife name Mary Lue Holt her nephew name Don Luna Gary Thomas Rowe FBI agents I never did learn their names. 2 police with the city of Birmingham my police nephew—C. Floyd Garrett my oldest sister's boy one deputy sheriff of Jefferson County name Hancock a CIA agent name Hubert Page they say is the best electrician the south made the electric switch that was supposed to have put their drip bucket bomb off that Sunday morning at 2 o'clock but the whole in their drip bucket got stopped up and didn't go off til just in time to kill those four young girls. Mary Lou Holt and Hubert Page got afraid and run away together. Went to Miami Florida. Stayed 3 months came back as man and wife . . .

That same letter included details of what Chambliss said happened the night when the bomb was placed. He claimed that officer Garrett made a phone call to the Birmingham Police Department, using a handkerchief over the mouthpiece to disguise his voice. According to Chambliss, Garrett had said he saw a suspicious-looking person at the Ramada Inn Motel and he might be placing a bomb. "He said I told Rowe now run hang you drip bucket at the nigger 16th Street Baptist Church. He said Mary Lue run her front bumper up against my back bumper as soon as Rowe hung his drip bucket they all run jumped in Mary Lue's car again."

He said Garrett led them away from the area, then pulled over and gave them the "highball" signal to go on. He quoted Garrett as saying, "I didn't care which way, just so they got their asses in the clear."

On another occasion he wrote a letter to Bill Baxley's wife. "Dear Mrs. Baxley," he wrote,

I hope and pray to God that you can help me and will and I pray anyone Doesn't Lie on your Boys and cause them to have to Die in Prison. Mrs. Baxley My Wife has had 3 Seorious heart Attacks since they Picked me up. They Like Not Have save her with the last one Mrs. Baxley I Will Tell you what My Lawyers told me Baxley sent His Investigators to Detroit Found this Colored Woman Who Would Lie on me For that Reward Then he flew up there in N.G. Plane Showed Her My Picture and the picture of Tommy Blanton's car Said this is the man that done the Bombing So.ans.soon..Yours Truly, R. E. Chambliss, Rt. 5, Box 125, Montgomery, Alabama 36109.

In 1979 he sent a letter to the new Alabama attorney general, Charles Graddick, saying that "Mafia Bill Baxley" and Art Hanes, Jr., had framed him and that Baxley had received kickbacks amounting to $175,000 from women who had been paid rewards in the church bombing. Chambliss wrote that one day he would get out of prison and would get even with those who had sent him behind bars.

Eddy had been convinced of Chambliss's guilt ever since hearing the stories of Elizabeth Cobbs and Gail Tarrant. But he had heard something else as well, something that to him was even more damaging—something that wasn't even said. One day while the trial was in progress he received a phone call at the courthouse. The caller identified herself as Robert Chambliss's wife, Flora. Eddy had never interviewed her. By law, she did not have to say anything against her husband. But she just wanted to talk to him, she said. Then she made a brief comment: "Well, if he's guilty, then I think he should be punished."

That was all she said. She never said he was guilty. She never said she saw him with dynamite. But she never defended him, either. She never said he was innocent.

Much mystery remained about who might have witnessed the klansmen putting the bomb down at the church. It seemed certain that there had been two women in a car who had gone to the Sixteenth Street Baptist Church during the night of September 14 and 15. One of those women, Eddy believed, was Gail Tarrant, and he suspected that the other was Flora Chambliss, who must have had a strong feeling that night that her husband was planning to bomb the church. He could only imagine that she felt she could not say anything to her husband directly and was probably afraid to say anything to police about him. But Gail Tarrant had relayed the story to the sheriff's deputy, Hancock, who had gotten around to acting on it too late.

On October 28, 1985, Chambliss was rushed by ambulance from the St. Clair Correctional Facility at Odenville to Birmingham's Lloyd Noland Hospital, a trip of about thirty-five miles. He was in critical condition. Before dawn on the 29th he was dead.

Whatever he knew about the most monstrous crime of the civil rights movement went to the hereafter with him. He never said anything about who might have been with him that night. Indeed, no member of the klan divulged one word about the bombing; none had broken the klan oath.

Funeral plans were made in secret by the family; the location of the service and burial were not revealed to the press. On the evening of his death, a Ku Klux Klansman, Roger Handley, called a reporter for *The Birmingham News* and asked how he could make contact with the family. "The klan does not want that old man to be buried as a pauper," Handley said. "All we ask is a chance to help."

The reporter relayed the message to the Chambliss family. A family member declined any help from the group. "If it hadn't been for the Ku Klux Klan," he said, "he wouldn't have died as a convict."

UNTIL JUSTICE
ROLLS DOWN

27

In the years following the conviction of Robert Chambliss, the bombing case faded from public awareness. The Alabama attorneys general who followed Baxley for the most part let it lie idle. Don Siegelman, who held the post from 1986 to 1990, once briefly revived the investigation, sending an agent to talk with Bob Eddy. Nothing further was heard from him after that one meeting.

As for the men who had been viewed as possible suspects in the bombing, life went on pretty much as usual. Thomas Blanton, Jr., was working in the sporting goods section of a Wal-Mart store in Birmingham, while Bobby Frank Cherry was retired and living in Mabank, Texas, about fifty miles southeast of Dallas. Cherry had driven trucks for several years and then took different jobs, including cleaning carpets.

Elizabeth Cobbs, the key witness in the Chambliss case, lived for some years in the fear that the KKK would seek revenge, sometimes telling friends she believed she was being followed. Then, in the mid-1980s, she underwent a sex-change operation and became known as Petric Smith. Smith/Cobbs wrote a book about the KKK's violent activity in Alabama during the 1950s and 1960s. It was called *Long Time Coming,* published by Crane Hill Press in Birmingham.

Bob Eddy, the investigator who led the probe for Bill Baxley in Birmingham, worked as an investigator for

Mobile County District Attorney Chris Galanos. He retired from that job in the early 1990s, and in January of 1995 he was appointed as Alabama's Assistant Director of Public Safety. Baxley, meanwhile, had long before settled into a successful private practice in Birmingham. His marriage to Lucy Richards ended in the mid-1980s, and in the spring of 1990 he married Marie Prat, a former reporter for the Associated Press.

By the late 1970s and early 1980s, Alabama officials began to give grudging recognition to the historic role the civil rights movement had played in the state. In Selma, where Martin Luther King, Jr., had led voting-rights marches in 1965, white city leaders began to take part in the planning of anniversary events. Tourists found a marked trail that followed the route taken by King's marchers. Selma police and Alabama State Troopers provided escort for memorial marches. In Montgomery, where the black boycott of buses in 1955 launched the modern movement for equal rights, the city began to use as its tourist theme the phrase that its history was linked to "the Civil War and Civil Rights." In 1979, when the KKK marched from Selma to Montgomery to "purify" the route made famous by the voting-rights march of 1965, Montgomery Mayor Emory Folmar and dozens of police officers and state troopers waited at the city line and arrested scores of robed klansmen.

In 1992 the city of Birmingham completed its Civil Rights Institute, located across the street from the Sixteenth Street Baptist Church. Mayor David Vann had first brought the idea of establishing a center to depict the civil rights movement in Birmingham to public attention in the late 1970s. About 95,000 tourists came to the facility the first year, and in the following years the number rose to nearly 150,000 annually, officials said. Most also went to the church to see the place where the bombing had occurred, to see for themselves the pictures of the four girls on the plaque. For many the church had become hallowed ground: it was more than a Birmingham historic site, more than a civil rights landmark; indeed, it had become an American shrine. A tour would take visitors from the front of the church to a section of the basement called the "memorial nook," where they huddled in clusters, talking in hushed tones. The plaque with the photos of the four girls was moved from its place near the altar to the nook. Across the street, in Kelly Ingram Park, sculptures reflect images of the civil rights struggle in 1963: figures of children marching, fire hoses and police dogs, a statue of Martin Luther King. In front of the facility is a statue of Fred Shuttlesworth.

The city itself evolved from a smoky, heavy-industry town to a center of higher education, medical research, and banking. The University of Alabama at Birmingham was becoming the largest single employer in the state. The downtown was given a new and more friendly look: trees and shrubs formed a divider along Twentieth Street, the main artery of commerce; sidewalks were widened; there was a glow of green throughout the business district. In the autumn the trees turned a blazing red-orange, while in the spring they produced thousands of white blossoms. It was a stark contrast to the hot streets of the 1960s.

The racial climate improved for African Americans; or, at least, it wasn't as bad as it had once been. The all-white police force had become desegregated, its racial makeup about 35 percent black. But like other urban areas across the nation, many middle-class whites and blacks had moved out of the city, most finding homes in the communities to the east and south. Hoover, a sprawling suburb, grew into one of the larger cities in Alabama and became the home of the city's minor league baseball team, the Birmingham Barons. The Barons had left Rickwood Field, a relic that was built in the early part of the twentieth century. And grand old Legion Field lost its most famous college football matchup, the Iron Bowl, Alabama versus Auburn. Both sites sat in the city's west side, an area that from the early 1970s had become mostly black neighborhoods.

But whites and blacks found themselves working together. Culpepper Clark, the dean of the University of Alabama's School of Communication, who often wrote about racial issues, said that whereas universities and corporations provided integrated social settings, schools and neighborhoods basically remained segregated. "It's not as good as it should be," he said, "but it's a lot better than it used to be. The separation is by choice, not by state law. It's good that we've done away with the days of the sixties."

One day in 1994 a meeting was held to talk about race relations in Birmingham. It was supposed to be an initial gathering for an exchange of ideas. The meeting was called by Rob Langford, the Special Agent-in-Charge of the FBI office in Birmingham. He invited some black ministers and other community leaders in hopes of smoothing relations between the bureau and the black community. In the early part of the decade the FBI spent a number of months investigating Mayor Richard Arrington, the city's first black mayor. There had been instances where Arrington had been tied into projects that appeared questionable. Many black residents thought the probe was racially motivated, and even though it ended without an indictment against the mayor, the sour mood prevailed.

Langford, fifty-four, had been assigned to the Birmingham office in 1993. Alabama was familiar territory to him. He grew up in Tuscaloosa ("I remember as you came into town there were signs of welcome from civic clubs and also one from the Ku Klux Klan") but opted to attend Auburn University. His wife, Martha, who also attended Auburn, was from Hueytown, a western Birmingham suburb. In 1962, after graduation from Auburn, he was commissioned a second lieutenant in the Marine Corps. In 1965 he was sent to Vietnam, where he eventually became the commander of an infantry company in the Third Marine Division. He was awarded a Bronze Star for displaying heroism when his company was attacked by a North Vietnamese battalion. After his discharge in 1968, he joined the FBI, having assignments in Houston and Detroit. He was later sent to Washington, D.C., where he was named an Inspector and also head of the Civil Rights Unit. He was then assigned as Special Agent-in-Charge of the Buffalo, New York, office.

One of Langford's goals in Buffalo was to foster a better relationship between the bureau and the black community. An invisible barrier had developed over the years, and Langford wanted to change that. He sent word to a group of African American ministers that he would like to meet with them. They responded with a visit to his office, which resulted in an amiable chat. A few months later, some police officers were charged with corruption. "Since the officers were black, it led to some in the black community saying it was a racial thing," Langford said. "But I contacted the ministers and we had another meeting. I was able to show them that the FBI had investigated many white public officials for corruption. So they were able to talk to the people in their neighborhoods and cool things down." Coming to Birmingham in 1993, he again set out to build a better relationship with the black community, given the city's racial history. One day in early 1994 he began his project, first contacting Birmingham Police Chief Johnnie Johnson for a list of names of leaders in the black community. Langford recalls:

[Johnson] came up with about twenty-five or thirty names, and I wrote a letter to each of them asking them for a meeting. Not one of them answered. So after a time I made telephone calls to them. Not one returned the call, not one. So I got to thinking, "Gosh, I guess I'm going to have to go visit them in person." And that's what I did. I went first to Lemarse Washington, a member of the National Conference of Christians and Jews. And then I went to see the Reverend Chris Hamlin, pastor of Sixteenth Street Baptist Church, and Eva Jones, principal of Powell Elementary School. Well, all said they would spread the word about meeting with me. So one day we all got together at my office. And they all sat there with their arms folded watching me. I told them I wanted them to be able to trust us, and for us to trust them. And I told them a little about the types of cases we worked, and that sort of thing. I wasn't even thinking about the church bombing. That wasn't even on my mind. So we had coffee and doughnuts and talked. Every one of them said the same thing: "This is the first time I've ever been to the FBI office." And some said that when they first got my letter they thought I was investigating somebody and wanted information. So, after a time the Reverend Abraham Woods spoke up and said, "Why didn't the FBI investigate the bombing of the church? The FBI never did do anything." I told him I thought we had, but I didn't know anything about it, that I was in the Marine Corps at the time.

I said I would look at it. And then he said, "These doughnuts aren't spiked or anything to make us talk, are they?" We laughed.

But I did have all the files on the bombing case brought into my office later, and in the months ahead I read them.

As he reviewed the boxes of files being brought in, Langford realized that the FBI probe had been massive. He said to himself, "Boy, there were a lot of people we talked to back then who would not talk to us because they were scared. Maybe after all these years, some of them will tell us what they know." Throughout the files he would find memos from J. Edgar Hoover with orders not to share information with the Birmingham Police Department or state police. There was distrust because of a belief that the KKK had infiltrated both agencies and that some officers sympathized with the Klan. Langford felt there was a strong chance that someone could shed new light on the case. The agents in 1963 had not been able to find a venue to indict. Langford also realized that if any new evidence did come out, it would be more of a state matter than a federal issue. Federal civil rights statutes had run out long ago, but under state law, murder had no statute of limitations. He went to see Jefferson County District Attorney David Barber. Barber listened to Langford, then said, "If you can get the material, I'll prosecute it."

Langford kept his project quiet, but he did call Reverend Woods and Reverend Hamlin to tell them, "The FBI had a huge file on the bombing case. I'm still looking at it. Just give me a couple of months to see what can be done." They said they appreciated the effort being made. Woods later recalled:

> I think the feeling of the black community toward the FBI went back to the 1960s, when agents would stand by and watch whites take part in racial violence against blacks and do nothing. Back then they would tell us they couldn't do anything, that they were just observers. But there was the whole thing of J. Edgar Hoover hating Martin Luther King and trying to get him to commit suicide. So there were other things. But the Arrington thing didn't help matters, although our feelings were more toward the Justice Department rather than the FBI. I believe I came on a little strong verbally towards Mr. Langford—Agent Langford, I always called him Agent Langford. But we later became friends. And it was Rob Langford who really got things rolling.

In the early spring of 1995, Bob Eddy received a telephone call at his Montgomery office. It was from Langford. He and Barber wanted to talk with him. "Come on down," Eddy said, not sure what they wanted. As soon as the two arrived, Langford began asking questions about the bombing. "I didn't know for sure what he was getting at," Eddy later recalled, "but before long it became clear to me that he was thinking about reopening the thing. He never said for sure." About a month later, Langford returned to Montgomery and talked with Eddy further about the case. Langford then told him it was going to be reopened. "He told me it would include the FBI, the U.S. Attorney's office, the

ATF, the local DA's office, the Birmingham Police, and the state," Eddy said. "But it was to be kept quiet; they wanted to keep it out of the newspapers and all the other media." Eddy went to Birmingham to attend the first meeting, which people from about a dozen various agencies attended. "The FBI later signed me to a contract to help out in the case," he recalled. "We had a number of meetings. In one of them they had Petric Smith, who had been Elizabeth Cobbs, come and answer questions."

28

——
——
——

Langford chose veteran agent Bill Fleming to be the FBI's point man on the investigation. Fleming was not enthused about the assignment. "I was not a happy camper," he recalled. "Man, this is a case that's almost forty years old. It has been investigated twice. We knew there were people out there that knew something, but who was going to come forward? The KKK? I felt I was being wasted. I felt they were throwing me on the trash heap." Fleming, fifty, was an energetic agent who sometimes wore his brown hair in a wavy perm. He had an overall rumpled appearance, and some of his co-workers compared him to the television character Columbo. It was a fairly accurate appraisal, for Fleming was relentless and became absorbed in the cases he worked. None would so deeply become a part of him as the church bombing.

A native of Albany, Georgia, Fleming joined the FBI in 1970 after serving two years in the Army. After he graduated from the FBI Academy in 1971, his first assignment was Kansas City, where he was with the stolen car section. Later that year he was transferred to Philadelphia. It was en route to that destination that he became deeply loyal to the bureau. He and his wife were driving to the new assignment with their second car in tow. The first night they stopped in East St. Louis, and after checking into a motel Fleming walked outside to get some items out of the vehicle.

I get outside and the cars are gone, both of them stolen. You know, you take one, you get the other. A lot of my personal belongings were in there. My FBI manual, my gun, a shotgun, and the watch my grandfather had owned. This was Thanksgiving week. I called the police and then the local FBI office. I figured J. Edgar Hoover would not be happy and I would not be employed much longer. In no time, it seemed, about a dozen agents were at the motel. They brought us money and clothing and whatever we needed. On Thanksgiving Day they were all out looking for my cars. They found them and arrested the guy. He had thrown most of my things into a trash dumpster. I got few of them back.

Fleming stayed in Philadelphia for seventeen years. Then, in 1988, he drew the assignment to Birmingham. In Alabama he worked various cases, including white-collar crime and civil rights issues, mostly involving charges against the local police.

Fleming's charge from Langford was to read every document the FBI had prepared over the years and see if a case could be made against anyone. Also assigned to the task was Ben Herren, forty-one, a detective with the Birmingham Police Department who would later be hired by the FBI. Herren was a trim, distinguished-looking man with gray hair and a mustache. Both he and Fleming wore glasses . . . and would need them in the coming months. The task of reviewing documents was a daunting one: there were over 140 files. The two developed a plan to interview the wives or girlfriends and relatives of klansmen as well as police officers, church members, and black residents who happened to be near the church that day. Fleming recalls:

I can't say enough about Ben Herren. He was steady, level-headed. When he first came to the FBI office he didn't have clearance to move around. I even had to escort him to the bathroom. But we gave him a cramped, windowless office to work in. And we had like eight thousand documents. We came up with the names of four informants, and we found that three of them were already dead. We thought some of the other people connected in some way might be sick and might want to leave a clean slate. That was absolutely not the case. Even some of the widows of klansmen were still scared, even though their husbands had died.

For more than thirteen months, Fleming and Herren read every bureau report they could find, learning about the players and looking for statements that could link someone to the crime. They followed up on a large number of people who had been interviewed by agents more than thirty years earlier. In all they cataloged the names of about five hundred people they wanted to interview. Many of those people on the list had died. Some of the women had remarried and changed their names. Others had moved. Many of those listed were in their seventies or older. A ninety-two-year-old man slammed the door in their face. Others claimed they could not remember anything about the case.

At times Fleming and Herren felt things were at a dead end, that it was folly to try to indict anyone, because there would not be testimony or evidence strong enough to support a guilty verdict. "I felt it was my responsibility to go to Mr. Langford and tell him that we could not prevail in court," Fleming recalled. "But he would tell me to keep on. Keep digging. And I knew that this was the last shot at this thing. It would never be investigated again. It could never be. Everyone would be dead. If we didn't do it, no one else ever would." It was reminiscent of words spoken by Chris McNair, the father of Denise McNair, to Bill Baxley in 1977: "I want you to go ahead. Because once you leave office, no one will ever try to do anything."

Langford, who would retire from federal service in 1996, was confident that somehow there would be a break in the old case. "Think how important it will be if you break it," he told Fleming. A break would not come before Langford's departure from the FBI, but in studying the files Fleming and Herren found that Thomas Blanton and Bobby Frank Cherry kept emerging as likely suspects, just as they had thirty years before. A decision was made to talk first with Cherry. Fleming and Herren asked their superiors if they could take Bob Eddy with them, since he had dealt with Cherry before.

Eddy, who had resigned his post with the Department of Public Safety at the end of 1995, had returned to his farm in Chilton County. On occasion he took on assignments as a private investigator, but mostly he tended to the task of raising cattle. Sometimes he went to art shows with his wife, Peg, who painted scenes of rural settings.

One night in early July of 1997, Fleming called Eddy at the farm and asked him to fly to Texas. Eddy agreed. They made the flight two days later and met with Cherry, who came to the Henderson County sheriff's office in Athens, about fifteen miles southeast of Cherry's home in Mabank. He had changed. He wore glasses, and the thick dark hair had become tinged with gray. But he said little, only that he had nothing to do with the church bombing. He remembered Eddy and reflected, "I thought you retired and was doing some farming."

"That's right," Eddy said. "I'm doing a little farming." Cherry, he noted later, seemed to have a good memory.

Then Cherry recalled the visit Eddy and Baxley had made in 1977. "I remember I slapped that Baxley," he said, chuckling.

"That's not true," Eddy said. "I was there. If you had done that, we'd have put you in jail."

Cherry maintained his innocence, and his best recollection of the night of September 14, 1963, was that he was home watching wrestling on television. But the FBI found that none of the Birmingham stations had aired wrestling that night (one must remember that in 1963 there was no cable television in Birmingham). Herren, who sat in on the interviews with Eddy, listened as Cherry explained his apparent defection from the KKK in August 1963, a month before the bombing. He told them that his wife had cancer and that he had to help take care of her. But later the FBI found medical records which showed that the cancer was not diagnosed until August 1965. The meeting did not seem to bear any results. Yet, a seed had been sown in the probe that was to bear surprising fruit.

29

On July 10, 1997, the FBI announced publicly that the case was being reopened. A federal grand jury was to be summoned to hear testimony from a number of witnesses. The announcement made banner headlines in *The Birmingham News* as well as the *Birmingham Post-Herald.* Meanwhile, filmmaker Spike Lee had been in the city to work on a documentary film about the bombing, called *4 Little Girls.* It would premier in Birmingham and later be nominated for an Academy Award. Some residents concluded that Lee's project must have played a part in the news that the case was being reopened. "That most definitely was not the case," Fleming said. "We were working on the case long before he came to Birmingham." The timing was mere coincidence, he said.

Meanwhile, in Texas, Cherry found himself the target of numerous visits by news reporters. At first they were angrily ordered off the property by either Cherry or one of his male relatives. But then, one day, he surprised everyone by calling a news conference. The news media showed up, and Cherry went before them saying he had nothing to do with the bombing in Birmingham in 1963. He hoped it would clear the matter up once and for all. Unfortunately for him, it backfired.

Among those who watched Cherry on television was Teresa Stacey, one of his granddaughters. She had heard something quite different from him earlier in her life. She waited a few days. Then she called the sheriff's office in Henderson County, Texas, which relayed her call to Fleming and Herren in Birmingham. They had a witness. Fleming said later, "That was the day we knew the thing had made a turn, and we felt there was a ray of hope that we might make a case after all."

Fleming and Herren continued their visits to former Klan members and/or their families and friends, trying to add to the case against Cherry. Several of those who were interviewed died shortly after, underscoring the fragile nature of the probe. Fleming would tell Carol Robinson of *The Birmingham News* that of the hundreds interviewed, fully 90 percent knew more than they admitted. "That was the sad thing," he told her. "They would lie to you with a straight face and their hand on the Bible."

But he and Herren stayed with it, and as they persisted, little by little, things began to fall into place. They found witnesses, and other witnesses came forward, calling FBI offices in different places to report that they had information on the bombing. A woman in Montana named Willadean Brogdon, who had once been married to Cherry, called the FBI office in Butte. She, too, had information, she said. "The media was our ally," Fleming said. "Every witness who bore positive information contacted the FBI based on media action."

On December 10, 1997, Doug Jones, forty-five, was named U.S. Attorney for the Northern District of Alabama. A Clinton nominee, Jones was a compact middleweight with thick brown hair that often touched his shirt collar. He had more than an average interest in the case; as a law student at the University of Alabama, he had come to Birmingham for the trial of Robert Chambliss in 1977. For him it was high drama, he said, almost like a movie unfolding before him, only the plot was real and the key players were not acting. He even told some of his classmates that one day he hoped to continue the search for others who took part. Now he was heading a grand jury looking into that crime which had retained its distinction as the worst single act of terrorism in the civil rights movement. Very rapidly the case for Jones became a mission, a journey to seek justice as well as to try to erase a stain from the city and state. Fleming and Herren were impressed with Jones's dedication, and he sometimes accompanied them on interviews.

Through most of 1998 there was little or no news from the investigation. However, the FBI assured reporters that the case was moving forward. Then, late in the year, a federal grand jury was called into session. The panel met at the Hugo L. Black United States Courthouse in Birmingham, a structure built in 1986. It was a beige-colored building with a plaza in front; the hallways and courtrooms were carpeted.

Among those summoned to testify before the grand jury was Cherry's oldest son, Thomas Cherry, forty-two, of Mabank, Texas. A tall, well-built man with thick dark hair, he was, like his father, a truck driver. At first he refused to talk with reporters. But one afternoon while waiting to be called to testify, he saw Peggy Sanford, a reporter for *The Birmingham News,* who was with another reporter. He nodded in curt recognition. She called to him, "Sir, can I ask you a question?" He shrugged, and she assumed that meant he would consider it. She introduced herself.

After a few basic questions, much to Sanford's surprise, Cherry suddenly began talking. "They haven't called me yet," he said. "I don't know what I can tell them. I don't know a whole lot. I don't know whether he bombed anything or not. He never said anything to me. But he was a tough man. I was still a kid in 1963. Once, when I was a teenager, he got mad at me, and I fell asleep on the couch. I got woke up when he hit me on the head with a two-by-four. Just hit me hard. It hurt." As he talked, Cherry began to tear, and soon he was wiping at his eyes. "I don't know if they'll ever get him to trial, he's in pretty bad health. This has got the family all tore up. He's had heart problems. I just don't think they'll get him to trial. I feel bad for those black families who lost their children that day." Listening to him, one got the impression that he thought his father might have been involved.

The grand jury met for many weeks, recessed for a time, and was later called back into session. One of the witnesses was Wyman Lee, a former Klan member and a close friend of Blanton's. In fact, he gave Blanton a job as a night watchman at his sewer-cleaning service, based at a junkyard, after Wal-Mart had dismissed Blanton from his job pending the outcome of the investigation. Unlike most former klansmen, Lee was a talkative man who seemed to like the press. But he did not have the kind of information that was tied to the case.

One night, three reporters for *The Birmingham News*—Tom Gordon, Jeff Hansen, and John Archibald—went to Lee's place to try for an interview with Blanton. Lee advised them that Blanton likely would not talk with them. They waited near the gate for several hours. Then, shortly before midnight, a car started up in the junkyard and headlights moved toward the entrance. The reporters stood in the driveway and waved. Blanton slowed the car but kept moving forward. Then he rolled down the window, leaned out, and called, "Get out of the way. You're in my way, step back." Then he drove past them and into the night.

In 1999, Petric Smith, who once had been Elizabeth Cobbs, the star witness in the Robert Chambliss case of 1977, died.

30

On May 16, 2000, Doug Jones and his colleagues went before a state grand jury that had been called at the Jefferson County Courthouse. They presented the evidence that Fleming, Herren, and other FBI agents had gathered. On May 17 the grand jury returned murder indictments against Thomas Edwin Blanton and Bobby Frank Cherry. Each was charged with eight counts of first-degree murder. Blanton and Cherry were charged with both murder and universal-malice murder. The latter charge meant they did not intend to kill a particular person but that the act clearly endangered anyone nearby. "This was a tragedy of just absolute monumental proportions," Jones told reporters. "It has scarred the city of Birmingham for almost thirty-seven years." He said he would prosecute the cases as a special Deputy District Attorney for Jefferson County. The jurisdiction was changed from federal to state, he explained later, because there is no murder charge that would cover the crime under federal law, whereas the state could bring murder charges.

After the indictments were handed down, Blanton and Cherry turned themselves in to the sheriff's department. They were booked at the Jefferson County Jail; bond was set at $200,000 each. A day later they were brought into a courtroom for a preliminary hearing. A front-page photo in *The Birmingham News* showed them in red-and-white candy-striped jail clothing. After so many years, the two, who had been under suspicion from the start, were charged with the bombing of the church. They entered pleas of not guilty. In the photo, Blanton appeared grim; Cherry's face wore a quizzical expression.

The men had already hired attorneys. Blanton was represented by David Luker, fifty-one, while Cherry's defense was to be handled by Mickey Johnson, fifty, and Rodger Bass, thirty-seven. Luker was from the Birmingham area, Johnson and Bass from adjoining Shelby County. Several court hearings were scheduled by Jefferson County Circuit Judge James Garrett, fifty-eight, who had served on the bench for nearly twenty years.

Johnson entered a motion on Cherry's behalf, saying his client suffered from dementia and was therefore incapable of understanding the charges against him or assisting in his own defense. Both defendants asked that the indictments be dismissed. Meanwhile, Cherry was able to post bond and was released. He took up residence in a mobile home in Shelby County on property owned by a relative. Blanton was able to make bond a few days later.

In the coming months there were a number of conferences and motion hearings. Then, in January of 2001, Luker resigned as Blanton's attorney, citing a conflict. In early February, Judge Garrett appointed John Robbins to represent Blanton. Robbins, forty-one, was born and raised in Trenton, New Jersey, and came to Birmingham to attend Cumberland Law School at Samford University. He graduated in 1987 and stayed in Birmingham. "The government had four years to prepare their case against Tommy Blanton. I had exactly sixty-six days to prepare his defense," recalled Robbins. "I know that because I counted them. I never did hear a reason why Mr. Luker was out of the case. It never came up. 'Conflict' can cover a lot of things."

Robbins would face prosecutors who not only had more time to prepare their case but also had a bit more experience. Jeff Wallace, forty-six, was a 1983 graduate of the Birmingham School of Law and had come into the case in July of 1997, just before the trip to Texas. He had been with the district attorney's office since graduation. Birmingham native Robert Posey, forty-nine, was a trim, dark-haired man who wore rimless glasses. A 1973 graduate of Washington and Lee, Posey spent several years in the Army, then began his law studies at Cumberland Law School, earning his degree in 1980. He was in private practice for a time before joining the district attorney's offices in Jefferson and Shelby counties. He became an Assistant U.S. Attorney in 1991 and had been brought into the case on October 9, 1998. In an interview, Posey recalled the day he was assigned to the case:

> I had heard that the investigation was being reopened, that we had opened a file. But I did not become involved with it at first. The first one to be assigned was John Ott, and he was with it for about a year. But John was appointed U.S. Magistrate. Then it went to two others, before I got the assignment. My first reaction? Well, it wasn't anything like, "Wow, I get to work on a historic case." No, it was more like, "Oh, great, a forty-year-old murder case. This will be a waste of time." I tried to recall my own thoughts about the bombing, but I could not remember much about it. I was twelve in 1963. I remember the murder of John Kennedy. It happened in about the same time frame, yet I couldn't recall a lot about the bombing. I just remember being aware that it had happened. But as I got into it, and got to meet the families and began to work with the evidence, I became more involved emotionally. I think anyone would get emotionally involved with this, especially someone who has children of their own. I have two daughters.

As the prosecution team worked on the case, they ran into numerous dead ends that were somewhat interesting but of little value to the attorneys who had to bring evidence into a courtroom. Typical was a day in 2000 that Jones, Wallace, and Posey went to the Birmingham jail. Police officers had called them after finding some material related to the case, they thought. The defense attorneys came along. They found an old metal file cabinet with an intriguing label that read "Bombing Cases." For hours they looked through the documents and found many letters written to former Birmingham police chief Jamie Moore, mostly from civic, business, and church leaders who approved of his handling of the 1963 demonstrations. There were also notes made by officers who monitored mass meetings in 1963, including comments on the speeches of Martin Luther King and William S. Coffin, a chaplain at Yale who spoke of civil rights for blacks. "It was fascinating reading," said Posey, "but of little value to the case."

Fleming, in the summer of 2000, came across an evidence inventory sheet on the bombing that was made in 1981. In it was an entry about tapes. He spent several hours trying to find them and finally located some reels in a locked file cabinet. The tapes had been there for a long time, but neither Bob Eddy nor Bill Baxley had known of their existence. The former attorney general, when told about them, became so angry that he wrote a long letter that was later published in the *New York Times*. If he had known about them in 1977, he said, he would have used them in the investigation and might have been able to get indictments against Blanton and Cherry at the same time he built a case against Chambliss.

Fleming and Herren checked into the origin of the tapes. They found that in 1964, FBI agent Brooke Blake had approached a KKK member named Mitchell Burns who lived in Blount County, just north of Jefferson County. Burns had agreed to secretly tape conversations in his car with Blanton. His decision to help was based on one thing: "The agent had shown him a picture of one of the girls killed in the bombing," Fleming said. "And he says, 'What can I do to help?'"

Burns now lived in Gardendale, in northern Jefferson County. Herren went to see him, but the former klansman refused to talk to a police officer and said he would talk only with the FBI. So Fleming went the next day to meet with him. He was met by a trim, silver-haired man who invited him in for a visit. Burns said he regretted his past ties with the KKK. As Fleming was shown into the house, he was surprised to see a figurine of a robed klansman in the kitchen. On the table was a handgun. Burns obviously did not trust strangers. But as they talked, Fleming told him about the murder charges against Cherry and Blanton.

Burns told Fleming about his activity for the bureau in the months after the bombing. In 1964, he said, the FBI asked him to make friends with Blanton. As luck would have it, Burns didn't have to go through with the ploy because literally out of the blue he was contacted by Blanton, who was being questioned regularly by the FBI. Blanton wanted to know if Burns could help get the agents off his back. It was the opening needed to start a relationship that would lead to the two of them driving around Birmingham, drinking and talking about women, blacks, and ultimately, about bombing things.

Burns said he had always used his car but insisted that Blanton drive, claiming he could not hold his booze very well. As they cruised the streets of Birmingham, they often talked about the civil rights movement. A number of times Blanton would drive by the church and Burns waited to see what he might say. The tape recorder had been installed by the FBI in the trunk of his car. The microphone was hidden behind the car radio, which had been disabled to prevent someone from turning it on and drowning out the dialogue. Still, the recorder did not produce a clear conversation. It did, however, pick up every pothole and railroad crossing in the city. Once, Burns said laughing, they drove by the FBI office and tossed out a cherry bomb. Fleming was fascinated. Then he asked Burns if he would testify at the trials. Burns said he would.

Jeff Wallace was assigned the task of preparing Burns for trial. In an interview with the author, Wallace said:

Mitch was a real likeable guy. He told me he got in with the Klan because they were drinking buddies, words to that effect. I said I thought he had done a brave thing by agreeing to tape-record conversations with Blanton back in the sixties. That really was a dangerous time. Anyway, the tape recorder he used back then was as big as a tire, and Mitch had it placed under his spare tire in the trunk. I said, "If you ever had a flat tire and some of those guys were in the car and saw that tape recorder, you would have been a dead man." Mitch said he knew.

Meanwhile, Fleming took another look through the evidence room and came across a second set of tapes, located on the fifteenth floor of the FBI office. At first he thought it was just a box of trash, but closer inspection revealed it was full of tapes of conversations between Blanton and his wife, Jean Casey.* Fleming and Herren listened to them and then listened again. They were not clear, but they were more damning to Blanton than the Burns tapes.

Fleming had found the second set of tapes almost by accident. Jones, Wallace, and Posey had gathered their witness lists and what evidence they had. By law they had to provide to the defense all information—called discovery—they had obtained. Posey recalls:

We were sitting in Doug Jones's office one day and we wanted to make sure we didn't leave anything out, so we asked the FBI agents to make one final sweep of their offices just to make sure we hadn't missed anything. So they come back later and say they found this box that had tapes in it. Fleming found them. There were a lot of tapes. Hours and hours of tapes. So we told them they were going to have to listen to them all. There had been a little note on the box that some agent had written back in 1964 when they were made that said something about the contents. And the word "bomb" was in there. I mean there wasn't an exclamation point or anything. But Herren and Fleming lis-

*They had married in Trenton, Georgia, on April 25, 1964.

tened and then brought it to us to hear, and I heard the word "bomb" and I thought this was great. But I wondered, how in the hell can we get this into evidence?

Actually, the tapes were almost an anticlimax, because I thought we already had a pretty good case against both of them. But the tapes were a very important addition to the case. They were of huge importance.

Called the "Q-9" tapes by the investigators, the recordings flip-flopped the thinking of the prosecuting team, says Jeff Wallace:

At first we thought our strongest case was against Cherry, not so strong against Blanton. But after we heard the tapes, we felt the best evidence would be against Blanton. At the time the tapes were made, Blanton was living in the west end section of Birmingham in the house that had been owned by his father, Pops Blanton. It had an addition built onto it, which was rented out. What Tommy Blanton didn't know in 1964 is that the person renting the apartment from him was an FBI agent. The tape recorder device was in the agent's apartment, but the microphone was placed in the space between the walls, which is neutral territory.

The apartment had been rented by FBI technician John Colvin and agent Ralph Butler. The recordings turned out to be high drama—and absolutely fatal to Blanton's defense. Although they were scratchy and jumbled with background noise—water running, pans rattling, people walking, boards creaking—the sound of voices could be distinguished. There was no forgetting the shrill tone of Jean Casey's voice: that of a woman demanding to know where her man had been one night some months before, and what he had been doing. On the tapes Blanton used the word "bomb" three times. The tapes would become the most damaging evidence against him.

Although no dates were mentioned, it was apparent that Blanton and his wife were talking about Jean being questioned by the FBI about Blanton's whereabouts on Friday night, September 13, 1963, and also the following night. It had been established that both Cherry and Blanton, as well as Robert Chambliss and several others, had been at the Modern Sign Company. There the group had made posters and signs to protest school desegregation orders by the federal courts. But it was also suspected that some of those there had other business.

One has to ask why the FBI didn't hear what was said on the tapes in 1964. According to Wallace, the agent assigned to monitor the tapes was also listening to another set at the same time and may have been busy when the two talked about the bomb. Also, the Blanton-Casey conversation only lasts a minute or so in the midst of hours and hours of silence with interludes of distant, garbled dialogue. It's likely that it was simply missed. Posey adds that the people working for the FBI in 1964 were no longer there in 2000, and the newer workers might not have known about the tapes.

Fleming had all the tapes sent to NASA, to the FBI's Washington headquarters, and then to a San Francisco company that specialized in digitally enhancing old tapes. He and Herren went on with their probe, doggedly sticking to their routine of finding and talking with people who might have even a remote tie to the case. Several of Cherry's family members made claims that he had mistreated them, and some of the women said they had been sexually abused years before. It was gritty stuff, but it didn't relate directly to the church bombing. Still, the allegations were pursued; Cherry was later indicted on the charges in adjoining Shelby County.

Judge Garrett, meanwhile, dismissed the motion to throw out the indictments and set Blanton's trial for April of 2001. At the same time he ordered that Cherry receive a psychiatric evaluation to determine if he was competent to stand trial. The defense attorneys made two other motions:

first, to have the case moved to another city; second, to deny prosecutors the use of the tape recordings. The judge simply denied the motion for a change of venue. On the second motion, Garrett set a hearing to take up the tapes issue. In 1964 and 1965, when they were made, tapes were allowed to be used for intelligence gathering but were usually not used in a courtroom as evidence. In 1968 Congress broadened the use of recording devices as long as a person's Fourth Amendment rights were not violated. After hearing both sides argue their case, the judge sided with Jones and his team, saying the tapes could be presented.

Prosecutors said the decision was based on the fact that on one set of tapes Burns had given his consent to be tape-recorded. In the other set, the recording had been made in a neutral space between walls separating the Blanton kitchen and the adjoining apartment. No one had trespassed onto Blanton's property to place the device there. Still, some legal scholars questioned whether the tapes should have been allowed in the case. It was an issue that Robbins would ultimately take to the U.S. Supreme Court. He says: "I don't believe the judge ever set out a written opinion on why he allowed the tapes, he just said he was going to allow them in. In 1964 tapes that were secretly made could be used by law enforcement only for intelligence gathering, but not in a trial. I don't know if Judge Garrett just interpreted the new law to mean it could be applied retroactively, or what. But he allowed them."

31

———
———
———

A revelation occurred at one of the preliminary court appearances: the identity of the informant known as Gail Tarrant. She was in reality Mary Frances Cunningham, the younger sister of Flora Lee "Tee" Chambliss. She was informing for the sheriff's department in 1963 and later reported to the FBI. Mrs. Cunningham had told the FBI in 1964—some reports say 1963—that on the night before the bombing she and Elizabeth Cobbs went to the vicinity of the church and observed a car that looked like Blanton's, in which were Chambliss, Cherry, Blanton, and a fourth man. The statement said Cherry was seen walking down the alley behind the church. He was carrying something, thought to be the bomb. She later called a sheriff's deputy, James Hancock. That phone call was made to his home in the early-morning hours of September 15, a few hours before the bomb went off. The deputy had hung up. Mrs. Cunningham said she met with Hancock after daybreak and that he later was en route to the church when the bomb went off. She would later deny everything. There was suspicion that in 1963 the two were romantically involved and that this was why Hancock was late—tragically, it turned out—in warning the church.

Fleming tells of going with Herren to talk with Mrs. Cunningham:

> She called us her angels, but I really fouled up when I asked her, "Were you and Hancock having an affair?"

Well, she reacted angrily and started rolling back and forth across the couch. I said to Herren, "I think I've upset her. Maybe I should leave and you continue." So I went outside and waited. Herren came out a short time later. There might be something to the story that she and somebody were down at the church that night. But if the thing about Hancock was true—and many think it is—that would be the second tragedy in this thing . . . that it could have been prevented. Why didn't Hancock just call somebody at the church and warn them to get out?

It was the same question Bob Eddy had raised in 1977. In the 1977 case, Baxley had decided not to call Mrs. Cunningham as a witness, because she was not reliable. Now, in 2001, Jones and his team made the same decision. But the defense attorneys sent her a subpoena. Mickey Johnson argued that the entire case against Cherry and Blanton was based on the statement Cunningham made to the FBI more than thirty-five years earlier. "She has denied making such a statement," Johnson told Judge Garrett in a hearing to dismiss the indictment, "but that statement has taken on a life of its own. And the state's case is flawed by the lie she told. The whole case is based on this false statement." Later he added, "I'm just suggesting that there are many other people the FBI should be looking at more closely."

Jones responded, "Judge, we've never said anything about Mary Frances Cunningham. We don't intend to call her."

As word spread about the true identity of Gail Tarrant, Cunningham found her house staked out by news reporters and television crews. A celebrity status was added when Connie Chung and her team showed up. Startled by the notoriety, Cunningham called the FBI, complaining that her property was becoming a sideshow and that she was virtually a prisoner in her own home. An FBI agent told her, "If they're trespassing, call the police." While Cunningham had not been a state witness in the first bombing case, Eddy maintains that she made an effort to prevent the tragedy that occurred on September 15, 1963. "She did everything she was supposed to do," he said. "She called a lawman and he did nothing. She was the only one who tried to do something."

Not long after Blanton and Cherry had been indicted, the state sent word to the defense attorneys that it might consider a plea bargain. Posey said there was a yearning for the whole story, to have the truth to come out about the bombing. If Blanton and Cherry did so, he said, the state would have been willing to negotiate. However, he said, neither man expressed any interest; thus no specific offers were advanced.

32

Blanton's trial began April 15, a warm, sunny day in Birmingham. While the preliminary hearings had been held at the Mel Bailey Criminal Justice Building, Judge Garrett decided that the trial would be heard in the old Jefferson County Courthouse, in the same courtroom where Chambliss had been tried in 1977. It was larger than the courtroom in the newer building.

The judge was also mindful of the news media, which consisted of about fifty or sixty individuals, including camera operators, sound personnel, and other technical staff, not to mention reporters. "We'll let you members of the news media stay up in the balcony," Garrett said. "That way you can move around and come and go as you need to. That be all right?" Most agreed because of the free access, but some preferred to find space on the main floor, which was packed with spectators.

Garrett was a husky man with thinning gray hair, gray eyes, and a prominent nose; his complexion had a ruddy tint to it; there was the look of an outdoorsman about him. He was receptive to reporters, and often during breaks in the hearings and in trial he was seen casually conversing with journalists or TV anchorpersons.

In the courtroom the first day, Blanton looked composed as he talked quietly with his attorney. He wore a blue-gray sport coat, dark blue pants, and a plaid shirt. He was clean shaven and appeared a bit younger than sixty-two. Although he occasionally glanced at the jury members, he

194

seldom turned to view the spectators. The jury was composed of eight white women, four black women, three black men, and one white man. Four were alternates. As the group came in, Blanton and the attorneys stood.

The media included Ken Sacks of the *New York Times* and Diane McWhorter, author of the book about Birmingham's civil rights era titled *Carry Me Home.* Howell Raines, editor of the *New York Times,* came to observe for a day. Rick Bragg would arrive later. Raines, Bragg, and McWhorter were all Alabama natives and Pulitzer Prize winners. *The Birmingham News* staffed the trial every day with two African American reporters, Val Walton and Chanda Temple. During lunch break one day Walton got on the elevator and was surprised to see Blanton and his attorney standing there. She dropped her pen, and before she could retrieve it, Blanton had leaned over, picked it up, and handed it to her without a word. The *Post-Herald,* Birmingham's afternoon paper, alternated reporters, usually sending Jamie Kizzire or William Singleton. Fred Burger represented *Newsweek.* Rick Journey would do an early-morning talk show for WBRC, then cover the trial. Donna Francavilla gave reports throughout each day for CBS radio. Jerry Mitchell covered for the *Jackson Clarion-Ledger,* and Glenny Brock got her first big story for the *Birmingham Weekly.*

In the first row of the downstairs section were members of the four girls' families. Sarah Collins Rudolph, the only girl in the women's lounge that day to survive, sat with her sister, Junie Collins Peavy. Nearby was Mrs. Alpha Robertson, in a wheelchair, and Chris McNair and his wife, Maxine. All were to be called as witnesses, but they were allowed to stay in the courtroom on agreement of the attorneys.

In opening remarks to the jury, Jones said the evidence would show that Blanton had been a part of the KKK conspiracy to bomb the church. Defense attorney Robbins called on the jury to listen to the evidence and reach a fair verdict. Tommy Blanton, he said, had been a "smart aleck" when he was younger. "He was a thorn in the FBI's side, annoying as hell," he declared, "but there's a lot of difference between that and being a bomber."

Also at the prosecution table were Posey and Wallace as well as Amy Gallimore, who handled press matters for the U.S. Attorney and helped out with witnesses. Judge Garrett told Jones to call his first witness. Among the first called to testify was retired FBI agent Charles Killion. Questioned by Jones, he testified that he was a member of the agency's laboratory in Washington and that he came to Birmingham on September 15, 1963, to look into the bombing. He testified that he knew from experience that it was a bomb and not an accidental explosion that caused the deaths and the damage to the church.

The Reverend John Cross testified much the same as he had at the first trial, that the Sunday school lesson for the service was "A Love That Forgives." He heard the explosion and saw smoke blow through the sanctuary. He thought at first a gas heater in the kitchen had exploded, he said, but then he caught the smell that was the same as firecrackers and knew it was a bomb. He told of helping find the bodies of the girls.

Alpha Robertson told how she heard the news of the explosion at the church. Maxine McNair spoke in a low voice about the death of her daughter, Denise. Richard Harris, a supervisor for the Alabama Gas Company, said that he had been called to check the gas lines and found them intact. It was not a gas explosion, he said. Church member Sam Rutledge described the frantic moments just after the blast. He testified of running to the side door and finding that the concrete steps outside had been blown away. He saw his Oldsmobile parked nearby and observed that it was badly damaged.

Mark Whitworth, an FBI agent, said the damage to cars was caused by the shock wave generated by the explosion. Fireman Jack Crews told of seeing the mutilated bodies of the girls. "It was bad," he said.

James Lay, the former captain in the African American arm of the Civil Defense unit who refused to testify in 1977 in the Chambliss trial, agreed to take the stand in the Blanton case. But just before the case was to be heard, Lay suffered a stroke and was unable to appear. However, the prosecution asked the judge for permission to read his responses to questions at trial. Garrett agreed, and Shelley Stewart, who was the radio voice to thousands of African Americans in Birmingham, read the Lay answers. In them, Lay said he saw two men who looked like Blanton and Chambliss approach the church on the night of September 1–2, 1963. Lay said he stopped his car and shouted at them, and they hurried back to their car. They were carrying something, he said.

Later in the trial, retired barber William Jackson testified that he had been affiliated with the KKK in 1963 and that he saw Blanton and Chambliss at the Modern Sign Company on Friday night, September 13, the night prosecutors believed the bomb was made. He also drove them to a KKK meeting held under the bridge on U.S. 280 at the Cahaba River.

On cross-examination, Robbins shouted at Jackson, "You're just a big fat liar, aren't you."

Jackson blinked a few times, then nodded, admitting that he had told some lies in connection with his association with the Klan. But he said he was telling the truth about Blanton being at the Modern Sign Company.

It was several days into the trial when the prosecution called Waylene Vaughn, who had dated Blanton in 1963. Now fifty-nine years old, she possessed a trim figure, her brownish-red hair touched with gray. Jeff Wallace questioned her.

"How long had you lived in Birmingham?"

"I was born here," she said.

She said that she had known Tommy Blanton in the 1960s. She pointed him out at the defense table.

"All right," said Wallace. "Were you and the defendant boyfriend and girlfriend at that time?"

She nodded. "More or less."

"Let me ask you . . . at that time were you familiar with

an organization that we might call KKK or the Ku Klux Klan?" asked Wallace.

"Yes." Then she added, "I never was a member," but she said she attended some KKK functions when Blanton took her along. "There were several at different locations," she said. "One was a Christmas party. They didn't wear their robes at that Christmas party. There were different meetings out in fields."

"Did you ever see Mr. Blanton in a robe?"

She had not, she said, but added that he seemed to be promoting membership in the KKK.

"Do you recall ever hearing him talk about explosives or bombing and that sort of thing?" asked Wallace.

"Oh, on occasion, he started explaining . . . about dynamite and how to connect the apparatus or whatever," she replied. But she said he never said he bombed anything. Later she testified about an incident that occurred when Blanton was driving her home one night. She said he drove by a black nightclub and threw a bottle at a group of patrons standing out front. Some of them chased their car, she said, and "they were going to beat the hell out of us," but when Blanton pulled a handgun and held it out the window, the group retreated. Another time, she said, he tried to run down a black man crossing the street.

She recalled seeing Blanton on the night of September 13, 1963.

"Do you know what time you got home?" Wallace asked.

"It was early the next morning," she said. "I don't remember."

Robbins rose for the cross-examination. "You knew he was a segregationist. Didn't you share his views?"

"No," she replied.

"Did you know you were going to a Christmas party?" he asked. "Isn't it true you wanted to be there?"

She shrugged slightly. "Not really."

"Isn't it true that you thought it was sexy—"

"No!"

"—to be at a Klan rally?"

"No," she repeated. "I always liked to observe people."

"You professed you're not a segregationist, not a racist . . . but you attend two Klan rallies—and a Christmas party sponsored by the Klan?"

"That's true."

"You didn't find the Klan sexy?" he pressed.

"Oh, God, no."

"But you hung out with Tommy Blanton," Robbins pursued, "and would shack up in motels around this town with him, right?"

She blinked several time. "If I want to put it that way."

"Well, I'm putting it exactly in your words," Robbins snapped. "You didn't like what he stands for, but you go to some hotel room and perform oral sex on him, didn't you?"

"That's correct," she said without flinching.

33

The tapes found in the FBI office—and the man who helped make them, Mitchell Burns—would provide one of the most dramatic moments of the trial. Fleming and Herren testified about the taping and explained how Burns, a former Klan member, had agreed in 1964 to have the tape recorder in his car. They told of the effort to get the old tapes copied and enhanced, as well as having transcripts made.

Jury members were given transcripts so they could read along as they listened. They were also given headsets to help them hear. Robbins objected to the use of transcripts and said the tapes had to be heard in their raw, original form, without someone preparing a written account. Garrett called the attorneys into his chambers.

"The relevance of the tapes starts on page one," Wallace told the judge. "He is always talking about harassing folks. And by the time we get to page two the defendant is talking about blowing somebody up. As we go through these exhibits you'll see reference after reference where the defendant has started talking about blowing something up or using dynamite. That sort of talk. Bomb this. Bomb that. The defendant is always bringing up bombing somebody." Robbins responded that he was on the record as objecting to the tapes.

Garrett allowed the tapes and transcripts into evidence, telling the jury they would have to determine the true relevance. Burns was called to the stand to testify about his undercover role in taping Blanton. Burns was seventy-four, a jaunty, silver-haired man who smiled as he took the witness stand. He wore a dark suit and a light purple shirt with a bolero tie. Silver-rimmed glasses framed a lean, tanned face, and his eyes sparkled with amusement as he began his testimony.

On questioning by Wallace, he said that he was in both the Marine Corps and Navy during World War II. He was sixteen in 1942, he said, and with both of his parents dead, he falsified records and enlisted in the Marine Corps. Later he went into the Navy. The Army, he said grinning, turned him down.

Robbins stood. "We object to going into his entire military record. We'll stipulate that he was a Marine."

When he came home from military duty, Burns said, he went to work for Hormel Packing House in Birmingham, working there twenty years. Then he became a mail carrier, working another twenty years before retiring. He said he had joined the Klan in the early 1960s, when he was thirty-five. He signed up with the Warrior Klavern. Later he joined the Tarrant Klavern.

After the church bombing, he said, the FBI repeatedly contacted him, but he refused to talk. Then one day in 1964, an agent, Brooke Blake, came to see him and showed him a picture of the four dead girls.

"What do you recall about those pictures?" Wallace asked.

"Well, it was the most horrible sight I have ever seen," Burns said. "Well, I told them I would do all I could to help."

He testified that the FBI installed a tape recorder in his 1956 Chevrolet, placing it under the spare tire in the trunk. He said he was paid two hundred dollars a month. When agents played the sounds for him in early 2001, he had to listen three times to be able to distinguish his voice from Blanton's.

The purpose of Burns's testimony was to lay the groundwork for prosecutors to play the tapes for the jury. The members were given headsets and a transcript of what was being said. The spectators could hear the tapes aloud, but the quality was such that much of it could not be clearly understood. Yet there was an eerie quality to it when one recalled that the recordings were made in a time of racial unrest and Klan terror in the South. Short phrases and words floated out over the courtroom as people leaned forward and listened in awe, glancing at each other with puzzled expressions.

"Nigger . . . damn church . . . bomb . . . damn niggers . . ."

And once, when it was recognized that the talk was about the bombing of the church, the voices crackled over the courtroom—as well as over the years:

"All this time I thought you were a clean-cut American boy," Burns says.

Blanton, his voice edged with merriment, says, "I am, I am clean cut. I like to go shooting, like to go fishing, like to go bombing. . . . Boomingham. Boomingham, that's my kind of town."

There is a reference to synagogues, and Blanton says, "They make the things dynamite proof, we'll have to go out of business. Or find something worse, you know, steal a atom bomb or a plane."

On the subject of chasing women, Blanton says, "I'm going to stick to bombing churches."

And Burns says, "Bombing churches, huh? You mean you get more thrill out of that than you do from women?"

"Hell yeah," Blanton replies. "They ain't gonna catch me when I bomb my next church."

"How did you do that, Tommy?" Burns asks, apparently referring to the September 15 bombing.

And Blanton answers, "Oh, it wasn't easy, boy, I'll tell you."

34

After a lunch break, Judge Garrett lost some of his good will. "This is addressed to the news media, particularly those that have cameramen out in the hallway," he said, his voice stern. "I have gotten several complaints about people being able to get around the cameramen. I've experienced that myself. If it happens one more time it will not happen again." He said he would remove them from the floor, adding, "A word to the wise is sufficient."

Then Burns returned to the stand.

Wallace asked, "Do you recognize your voice on those tapes?"

He affirmed that he did.

"And did you recognize the defendant Tommy Blanton's voice on the tapes?" Wallace asked.

"I certainly did," Burns said.

"Now we heard references to a man named Bob Chambliss," Wallace said. "Did you meet Bob Chambliss?"

Burns nodded. "I met Bob Chambliss."

"And a person by the name of Bobby Cherry. Did you meet him?"

Burns nodded. "Bobby Cherry."

"Now there were references to a cherry bomb being putting off, a cherry bomb," Wallace said. "Was there ever an occasion that the little firecracker device known back then as a cherry bomb was thrown out the window at different places?"

Burns nodded.

"Did y'all ever throw one at the FBI building as you went by it?"

Again the nod. "Behind it."

"Now, when you talk about dynamite or those other things," Wallace said, "you're not talking about cherry bombs, are you?"

"No, sir."

Burns testified that he always let Blanton drive. And Blanton, he said, would almost always drive by the church.

John Robbins's cross-examination of Burns would be grueling. It started out easy enough, with Burns getting confused on dates, saying he thought the bombing of the church was in 1964. Asked about KKK activity, he said he had taken part in several events. "We marched in front of a black nightclub in Jasper," he said, and he had been in Birmingham on May 14, 1961, when KKK members beat the Freedom Riders at the Trailways Bus Station.*

"You watched the Freedom Riders get beat up?" Robbins asked. Burns said he had watched, and added later that he was never a racist. "I never said nothing about blacks." He went on, "At that time just about everybody joined the Klan for a lark. I had close friends to join the Klan and never attend the first meeting."

"Wait a minute," said Robbins. "Let's get this straight. You joined the Klan just as a lark?

"That's right."

"Kind of a joke?" Robbins pursued.

"That's right."

Now Robbins's voice took on a mystified tone. "You joined as a lark and went out and got a robe and a hood? Did you think it was funny?"

"It was interesting."

"Well, I didn't ask you if it was interesting," Robbins snapped. "I asked you if it was funny."

---

*The Freedom Riders were a racially mixed group, mostly college students, who rode buses through the South in 1961 to see if the facilities were still segregated.

"I didn't laugh."

"It was interesting to watch folks beat up black folks?" Robbins pressed.

"I never seen no black folks beat up."

"Okay. You went down and watched the Freedom Riders get their heads busted in, did you?"

"Yes, I did."

"Did you think that was funny?"

"No, I didn't think it was funny," Burns said, his voice more serious.

Then moving to another area, Robbins asked about the FBI's initial contact with Burns. The witness said agents met him first in November of 1963. Then he was asked about a waitress at a restaurant in Blount County.

"Back then you had a little thing on the side with Marie Aldridge, right?" Robbins inquired.

To the surprise of spectators, Burns blurted, "I certainly did."

Robbins nodded. "Okay. You were having sexual relations with Marie Aldridge, right?" Burns stared straight at him. "I did not have sexual relations with Marie Aldridge."

Robbins shrugged. "You didn't have sexual relations with Marie Aldridge like Bill Clinton didn't have sexual relations with Monica Lewinsky?"

"No," Burns snapped. "I didn't use a cigar either."

The courtroom exploded with laughter.

It stopped Robbins for a moment. Then, "She was your girlfriend, right?"

"She was a good waitress," Burns declared pointedly.

Robbins changed the topic. "The FBI asked you to start ratting on Mr. Blanton, right?"

"They asked me to help them."

The attorney approached Burns and showed him a photograph, asking if he recognized the subject as Thomas Blanton. The picture was actually a side view of E. R. Fields, a leader of the National States Rights Party in 1963, who bore a resemblance to Blanton.

Burns gazed at the picture. "Well, to me, this man here, he was a better-looking fellow than Tom Blanton."

There was some low laughter in the courtroom. And Robbins asked, "You think he's better looking?"

Burns shot back, "You want to take a poll?"

There was more laughter, and Judge Garrett instructed, "Just answer the questions, Mr. Burns."

Robbins turned his focus to the nights the witness and Blanton would ride around Birmingham. "Well, you would go to many nightclubs together."

"That's right."

"And drank a whole lot of beer?" Robbins asked.

Burns shook his head. "My favorite drink was vodka."

"All right," Robbins said, a little impatiently. "You drank a whole lot of vodka, a whole lot of whiskey, right?"

"I don't like whiskey," Burns said. But he admitted doing a lot of drinking, adding, "The only way I could stand him was if I was half drunk."

"So in all these conversations you've had with Mr. Blanton, he's never told you that he bombed the Sixteenth Street Baptist Church, did he?"

"He certainly did not."

"You were only two good old boys out having a little fun?" Robbins asked. "And it was all said in a joking manner, right?"

"I was acting," Burns countered. "I don't know what he was doing."

"You were acting?"

"Yeah."

"You guys were laughing a whole bunch," Robbins said. "Made some pretty sick jokes."

The witness nodded. "Sick, sick, sick."

"And y'all talked about bombing, right?" Robbins asked. "Did you guys ever go out and bomb anything?"

Burns shook his head. "Me and Mr. Blanton never bombed nothing."

Robbins's voice was edged with cynicism as he asked, "Didn't you agree somebody probably should have told Martin Luther King, you know, his job would have been a lot easier if he just said Tommy Blanton was the only racist in Birmingham?"

"Objection," Wallace called.

But Burns replied, "No, I don't think so."

"Overruled, he answered," said Judge Garrett.

Wallace rose for redirect questioning. "Well, under those conditions, can you afford to get real drunk?"

"I don't think so," Burns replied, "because I wasn't drunk. I was scared to death."

"The last thing you're going to do is let yourself pass out in the car with this recorder back there?"

"That's right," he agreed.

Then Robbins was back on the floor. He showed Burns a statement he had signed for the FBI in 1964. He had written, "I missed a Klan meeting to meet with this punk."

"Is that your handwriting?" asked Robbins. "Is that what it says?"

Burns studied the paper briefly. "That's my handwriting," he said.

"And you're referring to Mr. Blanton, right?"

Burns shot a glance at the defendant. "He's the only punk I know."

Robbins smiled slightly. "And he never told you he blew up the church?"

"He certainly did not," Burns said.

"Okay. You made a whole lot of money to tell us that Mr. Blanton is a racist and a punk."

Burns gazed back at him. "I did not say he was a racist."

"But you got paid."

Burns shrugged slightly. "You know, sometimes we do things that we don't get money for, and this is one of them. I didn't make no money. I spent whatever I did for booze."

35

The Q-9 tapes, those made at the Blanton house on June 28, 1964, produced the most damaging evidence against the former KKK member. The packed courtroom remained still as Jones and his team prepared to present them. Jury members again put on their headsets, then read along as a transcript helped them follow the content of the recording. It started out with a hollow roaring tone. Then, suddenly, the shrill voice of Jean Casey was ringing over the courtroom. It was about the whereabouts of her boyfriend on the night of September 13, 1963. The FBI had questioned her about Blanton's alibis.

"Well, you never told me what you went to the river for, Tommy," she cries out.

Blanton replies, "What did you tell them I did?"

"You didn't ev—"

"What did you tell them I did?" he interrupts. "What did they ask you?"

"They asked me . . ." Here the words are garbled, and then she says, ". . . I said I didn't know."

"There. We were at the meeting," Blanton says. "I went to the meeting."

Her voice continues to reflect puzzlement: "What meeting?"

"The big one," he says in a matter-of-fact tone.

"What big one?"

"The meeting where we planned the bomb," he says.

She is clearly exasperated. "Tommy, what meeting are you talking about now?"

He answers, "We had the meeting to make the bomb."

"I know that," she says. "It's what you were doing that Friday night when you stood me up?"

"Oh, we were making the bomb," he responds.

"Modern Sign Shop," she says, trying to nail down where he was.

"Yeah," Blanton says. And then, in the same flat tone, he switches topics, saying, "I think I'll wear this sh—I think I'll wear this shirt."

36

The crowds at the trial would be shoulder-to-shoulder at times, but on some days there were just a few spectators. One afternoon, Art Hanes, Jr., who had been the defense attorney for Robert Chambliss in the 1977 trial, walked into the balcony during a recess. Hanes was now a circuit judge. He was asked if he had any thoughts on the trial.

Hanes grinned and shook his head. "I don't think a judge should be making comments about an ongoing case." He shrugged. "I just came to get a look at the place," he said. Then after a few moments, he commented, "It smells the same." After a pause, he said, "Well, I've seen enough." He walked out.

On a Saturday morning, Dan Wright, a dentist, found himself a place in the back of the balcony. "I just wanted to see a trial that is part of history," he said.

One of the last witnesses for the prosecution was Chris McNair. He had been on the front row for the entire case. As he went to the witness stand, Jones stood, then asked about that Sunday morning in Birmingham.

McNair recalled that he was at St. Paul Lutheran Church. He told of going to the hospital after he heard the explosion. There, he said, he found his daughter, Denise, in a makeshift morgue. McNair's testimony was quiet, calm.

"Mr. McNair," Jones said, "was there anything . . . was there any debris or anything on Denise?"

"Yes."

"What, if anything, in particular?"

"There was a piece of mortar mashed in her head right in there," he answered, pointing to a place on his own head.

"And was that at the time that you observed in her . . ." Jones paused, picked up something from a table, and showed it to the witness. "Do you recognize that?"

"It's a piece of mortar," McNair said.

"And that was what was given to you by someone at the funeral home?" Jones asked.

"Yes."

Sarah Collins Rudolph, the lone survivor in the lounge that day in 1963, retold her memory of the blast and of vainly shouting for her sister, Addie.

Robbins did not cross-examine either McNair or Mrs. Rudolph.

Blanton's defense was sparse, with only two witnesses called. That surprised some who felt there was an outside chance he might take the stand to claim his innocence. In an interview with the author, Robbins explained: "Of course, you always think about the defendant taking the stand. But we felt there was no real need to. And besides, the government had years to gather material to cross-examine him on, and I had eight weeks. So we did think about it, but we decided not to. In the end it was his decision."

Robbins first called FBI agent Bill Fleming to testify about the car James Lay had seen on the night of September 2, 1963.

"What kind of car did Blanton own?" he asked.

"A blue-and-white Chevrolet," Fleming said.

He then said that Lay had told agents he had seen two men who looked like Blanton and Chambliss on that night and that they were in a black 1957 Ford.

"Okay, Mr. Blanton did not own a black Ford, correct?" Robbins asked.

"That's correct," Fleming said.

"And Mr. Chambliss did not own a black Ford, correct?"

"That's correct."

"And in your investigation of this case, was a black Ford seen at Dr. Fields's house?"

Fleming nodded. "It had been seen at his residence, yes sir."

Fields had been a leader of the National States Rights Party. Robbins was raising the point that someone other than Blanton could have been involved in the bombing.

Doug Jones cross-examined Fleming briefly. The agent recalled that Lay did not say the two men he saw that night merely *resembled* Blanton and Chambliss. He had positively identified them.

The second defense witness was Eddie Mauldin, Jr., a black man who said that he was standing about a block from the church the morning of the bombing. He was seventeen at the time.

"Where were you in relation to the church when the bomb went off?" Robbins asked.

"I was on Sixteenth Street between Seventh and Eighth Avenue," he said.

Mauldin said he saw a Rambler station wagon, dark blue on the bottom, light blue on top, drive slowly along Sixteenth toward the church. He said there were two Confederate flags on the front. There were two young white men in the car, one of them with a tattoo of an anchor on his arm. He said the car resembled his father's 1957 Chevrolet, except for the paneling on the side.

As the car had neared the church, he said, the bomb went off and the car sped away, turning east on Sixth Avenue. "It seemed like all of a sudden it just burnt the rubber turning the corner." Some witnesses had told the FBI that earlier that Sunday morning they had seen a blue-and-white car with one man in it and one Confederate flag flying from the rear antenna. Mauldin's testimony raised the possibility that someone had thrown a bomb at the church.

The defense then rested its case, and Judge Garrett ordered a break as the attorneys prepared for their closing argument. Stepping outside for a moment, Robbins was asked by a reporter, "What's the best outcome you hope for?"

"A hung jury," the attorney quickly replied.

"Really? Does your client know that?"

Robbins nodded. "He knows it."

37

Robert Posey gave a dynamic and dramatic closing argument, pausing on occasion for the facts to sink in. The jury members were riveted by the low-pitched delivery.

"Thank you for the attention you have given to the presentation of evidence," he said. "I want to talk to you about the indictment against this defendant, and about why the evidence proves that he is guilty. There are four indictments for the murder of four little girls: one for Cynthia Wesley, one for Carole Robertson, one for Denise McNair, and one for Addie Mae Collins. Four little girls—in church—on a Sunday morning."

He then showed slides of the girls. There was silence in the courtroom as the pictures flashed on the screen. Then the screen had the image of Sarah Collins, the lone survivor in the lounge.

"There was a shock wave of excruciating pain that swept over Sarah Collins as she lay in the rubble of the women's lounge, blinded in both eyes, crying out for her dead sister, Addie," Posey went on. "There was a shock wave of grief that swept over the McNairs, and the Wesleys, and the Robertsons as they learned that their children had been senselessly murdered. There was a shock wave that swept all across the Earth, as the world learned of a horrible crime committed in Birmingham, Alabama. The question on so many lips on September 15, 1963, is a question still before this jury today. Why? The grand jury that returned the indictments charged that this defendant killed these children unlawfully and with malice or criminal intent; and the grand jury also used this language . . ." And here the jury again saw pictures of the devastation caused by the explosion. Posey continued, using the grand jury's wording in the indictment: ". . . 'by setting off or exploding or causing to be set off or exploded dynamite or other explosive, at, under, or dangerously near, the Sixteenth Street Baptist Church, during Sunday morning church worship services . . .'"

He then briefly recounted the testimony of FBI agent Charles Killion, who recognized an explosion caused by dynamite or other agent as opposed to an accidental blast set off by natural gas. He spoke of the tapes, which had played such a crucial role in the state's case. "We went to a lot of trouble to try to figure out each word," he said, "because we thought it was important to have a transcript that was as accurate as possible. Transcripts help us to understand what is said on the tape. This is a tape of Blanton's confession of guilt in this crime."

Then he went over the conversation between Blanton and his wife, when the defendant said he had attended a meeting where the planning for a bomb was done, and a meeting where he said "the bomb" was being made.

"How do we know that 'the bomb' is the Sixteenth Street Baptist Church bomb?" Posey asked. "For one thing, 'the bomb' could have only one meaning in Birmingham, Alabama, after September 15, 1963. We also know that it was around September 15, 1963, that Blanton was seen with Chambliss and other klansmen at the Cahaba River bridge, and at the Modern Sign Shop."

Then Posey asked the question that had been raised probably a million times in the years after 1963. "Why would anyone bomb a church? Who would have a motive to commit such a crime? The grand jury's indictment touches on this question. The grand jury charged that this defendant killed these children 'by perpetrating an act greatly dangerous to the lives of others, and evidencing a depraved mind regardless of human life, although without any preconceived purpose to deprive any particular person of life.' This defendant didn't care who he killed, as long as he killed somebody, and as long as they were black.

"Who would do such a thing? The same man who rode around Birmingham committing random acts of violence against black people. The same man who we hear on tape saying, 'They're not gonna catch me when I bomb my next church.' The same man who, even a year after the horror of September 15, 1963, can be heard on tape cursing the name of the church where these children died. The same man who lied to the FBI about the Klan, and about what he was doing that Friday and Saturday night before the bombing. The same man who, when his wife asks, 'What did you go to the river for?' says three times on tape that he was at a meeting where they made a bomb. That same man is seen at the church, with Chambliss, in the middle of the night, with a satchel in his hand, at the very spot where the bomb exploded that killed these children. Ladies and gentlemen, this is the man who committed this crime."

On the screen, there were photos of the victims. "This is Cynthia Wesley," Posey said. "This is Carole Robertson. This is Denise McNair. This is Addie Mae Collins. This defendant killed this beautiful child because of the color of her skin. He murdered these four worshipers in God's house on a Sunday morning, because he was a man of hate!" The word was shouted, and hung over the room for a moment. Posey continued: "The hatred, the intolerance, the injustice perpetrated by this defendant must not stand unchallenged."

He then touched on the testimony of Waylene Vaughn, recalling what she said about going with Blanton to KKK meetings, where men wore hooded robes and shouted their messages of hatred.

"And he explained to her about dynamite and fuses," he said, "and he talked about wanting to kill black people. And he had names for black people, and they were hateful names, profane names."

Then Posey recounted the testimony of Mitchell Burns. "He was a crusty old former klansman. But he was also a man with two daughters. And he saw photographs of four little girls laid out on a slab at a morgue, and he told us that it was the most horrible thing he had ever seen. He agreed to do a brave thing. He agreed to help the FBI investigate a murder suspect. As he rode around night after night, he must have wondered what would happen if this murder suspect discovered the tape recorder in the trunk of his car. But he kept doing it, and he collected evidence that tells volumes about the mind of this defendant."

Posey concluded: "The deaths of these four little girls must not be in vain. Don't let that happen. Don't let the deafening blast of his bomb be what is left ringing in our ears. Don't let it drown out the voices of these children. On behalf of the State of Alabama, and on behalf of these four little girls, I ask you to find this defendant guilty as charged."

38

In his closing argument for the defense, John Robbins took aim at the character of some of the witnesses for the state. He challenged Waylene Vaughn's contention that she was not a racist in 1963.

"Now she comes here and says some really bad things," he told the jury. "She says Tom Blanton is a bad man, okay. But she continued to date him. If he is such a bad man, I mean, come on. You saw pictures of him. He's not that good looking. And, by God, he didn't have any money. I mean she keeps going . . . she wants to come out on one side of her mouth and say he's such a bad person. Doing all these things to black people. Never reported one. Never been corroborated. Not one of those claims has ever been corroborated."

And then there was Mitch Burns, he said, an informer paid by the FBI to tape-record conversations with Blanton when the two were drinking. "You probably knew people like Mitch Burns," he confided. "Turn informer for money. Two hundred bucks a month."

He paced in front of the panel as he let the words settle in. Next he took aim on William Jackson, the barber. He chuckled for a moment. "This is my favorite witness, I guess. William Jackson. Now if you believe William Jackson is anything but a liar, then raise your hand and say let's stop now, go back and convict my client. If you believe he's anything but a liar." Robbins said Jackson's accounts of various events differed greatly with each telling.

"He gave numerous statements in the 1960s and said that it was Friday night the thirteenth [of September 1963] that he saw Blanton and Chambliss at the Modern Sign Shop," he said. "He didn't change it to the fourteenth until he checked himself out of a psychiatric ward in the 1970s to meet with Bill Baxley. And then, 'Well maybe I'll move to the fourteenth' because he really wanted that reward money. He's still P.O.-ed to this day that he hasn't gotten any reward money." Then, he says, Jackson testifies about Blanton and others being at the Modern Sign Company where a bomb was planned and made. "What did they do?" he asked. "Make a bomb, then unmake it, so they could put it together again?" Such a chain of events made no sense, he said. If there is reasonable doubt, he said, the jury must acquit his client.

Robbins further used the testimony of Eddie Mauldin to raise the issue of doubt. It could have been two white men in a Rambler who bombed the church, he said, suggesting that they could have thrown a bomb from the car window. And he challenged James Lay's statement about the type of car he saw one night at the church, a black 1957 Ford, the type driven by Ed Fields. Blanton drove a blue-and-white Chevrolet. Such things could raise a doubt about the state's case.

In his closing, Doug Jones zeroed in on the tapes made in 1964 at the Blanton home at 1440 Princeton Avenue. All the evidence came together, he said, falling into place.

"Planning the bomb. The Cahaba River. The meetings that were held. The Modern Sign Shop. Robert Chambliss. September the second. James Lay. They all come together. Are there some pieces missing?" he asked. "Yes. Can we see clearly the picture? We can see clearly the picture from Tom Blanton's own mouth. And ladies and gentlemen, we come here, in this time and place, to do justice. And it's not cheapened. It's not been thrown about. It's real. And we come here because there were four children who died and the world changed and we changed. And we come here because a mother's heart never stops crying. And we come here because we do remember. And every day that passed and every year that passed and Tom Blanton gets older is a mockery of the death of those little children. Every year that passes, bigotry and hatred proliferate. And every year that passes, some child can cringe in fear that maybe if I go to Sunday school today I won't come home. Ladies and gentlemen, there are a lot of people looking. There are a lot of people, but there's only four that matter: Denise, Cynthia, Carole, and Addie. Those four are the people that look down for the hope and inspiration. Those are the people that look down for justice. Because as Sarah called out, 'Addie, Addie, Addie' in cries of pain, today let us call out to Addie, let us call out in joy and happiness to Addie and her friends . . . that today, in this time and in this place, we did justice. And at long last—it has been a long time—but at long last they can rest in peace because it is never too late for that. And Tom Blanton can finally be held accountable for the crime he committed in 1963."

On the afternoon of May 1, 2001, the jury began its deliberations. Then, when they had left the courtroom, Judge Garrett was asked by several reporters if they could listen again to the tapes and perhaps use the headsets, just as the jury had. The attorneys did not object, and the group moved forward.

Some of the spectators, those who had been there for most of the trial, moved to the front and availed themselves of the equipment. For those who did not get a headset, the sound system carried the words over the courtroom. But there was so much talking that it was still difficult to clearly tell what was being said. In fact, even those with headsets still had puzzled expressions as they listened. In fact, some of them did not hear anything at all because one of the attorneys had left a briefcase on the table. It blocked the signal from an electronic device that was necessary to carry the transmission.

Then began the long wait for the verdict. No one ever knows for sure how long a jury may require to reach a decision. Jones and his team retired to his temporary office in the courthouse. Spectators and the news media sat in the courtroom for a time, then gradually trickled outside to catch some fresh air or find a restaurant nearby. A few tried to guess how long the jury would be out. It was getting late in the afternoon, and shortly after 5 P.M. the word began circulating that the jury was not going to reach a verdict. They planned to eat dinner and then retire for the night. One TV station put out a special report for its viewers that there would be no verdict. Some reporters began to drift back to their hotel rooms or offices to file stories.

Jeff Wallace and the other prosecutors heard the same thing, and Wallace got up and left the office, trying to analyze what it meant. Were they just tired, or was there already someone sticking fast to a not-guilty verdict? In an interview, Wallace recalled his feelings at that moment:

> We got a call from the bailiff who said the jury was going to retire for the night. They were staying at the Tutwiler. So we figured that was that. I didn't like it, because I wanted a jury to make a decision before going home. I felt our chances wouldn't be as good the next day. Anyway, I walked over to the courtroom and I was just standing in there, thinking about the case, wondering. I was there for a few minutes, and about that time one of the bailiffs saw me and says, "We got a verdict." And I was, I guess, a little scared. And about that time Doug Jones came in and I said, "We got a verdict." He didn't breathe. His face turned white. I think I was overcome a little with the emotion, that here in this courtroom where I had graduated from law school, that this trial was coming to its end and I was a part of an important thing. I remember thinking, they cannot find him not guilty. But at the same time, the case was so old that I didn't know.

By then the word was bouncing through the halls that a verdict was in; the news media and spectators, some carrying newspapers and books, jostled through the hallways and squeezed into the courtroom. The place was coated in stillness; only the sound of the shuffling feet of the jurors was heard. When all were seated, Judge Garrett asked the foreperson if the group had reached a verdict.

They had. It was guilty on all counts.

There was a collective intake of breath as the spectators reacted. Tom Blanton stood looking at the judge, perhaps not quite believing what he heard. He was asked if he had anything to say before sentence was imposed. He did not. Garrett said the sentence was life in prison. Then Blanton was taken by deputies who snapped the handcuffs on him and rushed him—it appeared to some that they were running—out of the courtroom and down the hallway to a waiting cell. It was over.

Afterward, in the bedlam, the reporters and television cameras surrounded Jones. Fleming and Herren stood behind him, as did Posey. Wallace stood on the perimeter. He had not talked to reporters during the trial, but now, since it was over, he decided he could answer questions. A TV cameraman and reporter came over to him. "Tell me your name," the reporter said.

"Jeff Wallace."

There was a pause. "Well, who are you?"

Wallace laughed. "I must not have impressed you. I'm part of the prosecuting team."

"Oh, okay." Then they hurried on to find bystanders to interview.

One of them, Willoughby Anderson, twenty-two, a Mountain Brook resident and Harvard graduate who had written a thesis on the church bombing, shook her head. Even with a guilty verdict, she said, "I just don't think there can be justice after thirty-five years."

Robbins filed a motion for a new trial, a preliminary step to an appeal. He raised some compelling points in his arguments before Judge Garrett, points that would be weighed by higher courts.

One was that the tapes made at the Blanton home were

"clearly not admissible." He argued that there never had been a document presented that showed the bugging of the Blanton home had been approved by J. Edgar Hoover, "in the interest of national security." He added, "All the evidence in trial was known to the government in the sixties. The tapes were clearly inadmissible in 1964–1965. The tapes alone led to the conviction."

Robbins also maintained that the state had discriminated against Blanton by using its sixteen strikes in jury selection to remove whites, including ten white males. Further, he said, one woman, who was selected to be the jury chairperson, slept through much of the trial. "We all know, as officers of the court, that she had slept through the trial," he said. Finally, he said, before the trial began, Mitch Burns had given an interview to a national television network, which could have influenced potential jurors.

Jones, in response, said he was not aware of a juror sleeping, and all the strikes in jury selection were race-neutral. He said one discriminatory strike was made of a white man who had tattoos. "I'm tattoo-impaired," he said. He said Robbins had done an admirable job in defending Blanton, especially since he had only eight weeks to prepare. To which Robbins responded, "Doug Jones and I have been friends for a long time. He is not going to get up and say anything other than that I did a good job. That's sort of like, you know, peeing on my leg and telling me it's raining."

The Alabama Court of Criminal Appeals and the Alabama Supreme Court turned him down, but there still remained the U.S. Supreme Court.

39

Jones and his team did not immediately turn their attention to Bobby Frank Cherry once they had successfully convicted Blanton. Cherry was still undergoing tests to determine his mental status, and there was a general feeling that he might not come to trial at all. Now past seventy, he was in generally poor health, and some family members felt he might die before any legal proceedings could ever begin.

But in the summer of 2001 there was a clamor in the black community that justice demanded he stand trial. The clock was running, they said. James Lay, the onetime Civil Defense captain whose testimony was read in the Blanton trial, died in June. There was a feeling of urgency about getting on with a trial for Cherry before more figures in the case passed away, including the suspect.

In the sultry heat of a July afternoon, about a thousand people, most of them black, gathered at Linn Park, a woodsy area between the courthouse and city hall, and held a rally calling on Judge Garrett to name a trial date for the former klansman. Reverend Woods, who had first set events in motion at that meeting with Rob Langford of the FBI in 1994, stirred the crowd with his fiery demand to bring Cherry into a courtroom. "If you have to carry him on a stretcher," he shouted, "bring him in to stand trial. We want him to face justice." And the crowd cheered. Then Woods and others led a march to the Sixteenth Street Baptist Church. There, speakers cried out for the need to try Cherry for the murder of the four girls.

Garrett was ostracized by some who believed he was protecting the man who once was a part of KKK nighthawk operations, a man who publicly admitted beating Fred Shuttlesworth in 1957. That incident occurred when the minister tried to register his two teenage daughters in all-white Phillips High School in Birmingham.

Meanwhile, the judge had ordered that Cherry be sent to the state's mental health facility at Tuscaloosa to be evaluated. Four psychiatrists examined him, questioned him, and gave him tests. After more than two months there was a mixed opinion about his condition. Most felt he suffered a degree of mental dementia, but some believed he was competent to understand things, and even smart enough to fake being mentally ill. Finally, in early 2002, Garrett ruled that Cherry was able to stand trial. It was set for May.

Cherry's attorneys, Mickey Johnson and Rodger Bass, had earlier filed a motion to have trial moved because, they said, *The Birmingham News* and the *Post-Herald* had between them published a total of 180 articles about the case. They also noted that, in addition to local newspaper stories, Spike Lee's movie *4 Little Girls* had probably been seen by some potential jurors, not to mention Diane McWhorter's book *Carry Me Home,* a Pulitzer Prize winner, in which she had written extensively about the case and Cherry. But Garrett denied the motion, noting that most of the people in the jury pool said they had not been influenced by the news media. Jones added, "With all due respect to Ms. McWhorter, I doubt that many jurors have read her book."

By March of 2002, prosecutors were lining up witnesses and preparing their strategy. Jones, who was no longer the U.S. Attorney, was appointed special prosecutor by Alabama Attorney General Bill Pryor. Meanwhile, Posey had enlisted the help of Deputy U.S. Attorney Don Cochran. Cochran was eager to be a participant, saying something to the effect that he'd tote water or be a "gopher" for the others just for a chance to be involved. He advanced the idea that while it might be hard to prove Cherry placed the bomb, a strong case might be made that he aided and abetted in the plot.

Cochran, forty-two, a native of Missouri, earned his law degree at Vanderbilt in 1992 after putting in nine years in the Army. As an infantry captain, he led a company of the 101st Airborne Division (the "Screaming Eagles") on a multinational peacekeeping mission in the Sinai Desert. He later became a detachment commander of a Green Beret "A Team," leading special missions in various locations around the globe, including the Middle East. Before joining the U.S. Attorney's office in Birmingham, Cochran had been a Deputy District Attorney in Jefferson County, specializing in murder cases. He prosecuted twenty-five of them, including several capital cases. His wife, Sandy, was president and CEO of Books-A-Million. In an interview with the author after the trial, Cochran reflected:

> I knew that the case was being investigated again while I was still at the District Attorney's office. I was keeping up with it through Jeff Wallace. I wanted to be involved. I was fascinated by it. In October of 1998, I joined the U.S. Attorney's office and for the first six months worked on civil cases. I volunteered to do anything in the Blanton case, do research, whatever. I did make the statement about even carrying water for the others. But after the Blanton case was finished, there were changes. George Bush had been elected president, and Doug Jones, a Clinton appointee, stepped down as U.S. Attorney. So the Cherry case was in the air. He [Cherry] was being evaluated on his mental condition. When it was decided that he was going to be tried, Robert Posey was in charge. One day he came to me and said, "Will you help me prosecute Cherry?" And I said yes. The history of the case was overwhelming. The four little girls were truly innocent victims.

Judge Garrett chose to hold the trial in the Mel Bailey Criminal Justice Center rather than at the Jefferson County

Courthouse where Blanton's case had been heard. The center was newer, though smaller (Rick Bragg of the *New York Times* quipped, "It's like having the trial in a double-wide.")

Reporters asked Posey how strong the case against Cherry was, and he replied, "Just wait and listen. All the parts will fall into place." And Cochran added, "We've put our hearts and souls into this."

The prosecution team produced witnesses who had heard Cherry make incriminating statements. Most of them had called the FBI when they first heard that the case was being reopened. The tapes, which had played such a pivotal role in Blanton's trial, would be used again by the state. There was one thing connected to the Burns tapes that was not admitted into evidence, Fleming said. One evening in 1964, an FBI agent went over the night's events with Burns shortly after he returned home. Burns told the agent that he and Blanton had gone to Cherry's house. On the way, he said, Blanton remarked that he was lost. Then Burns reported that Blanton said something akin to "I got lost coming up here before," saying it was the night the bomb was put down at the church. The words were not on the tape, or at least were not clear, and Garrett ruled prior to trial that it could not be admitted.

The jury was selected, composed of sixteen members, four of whom would be alternates. As in the Blanton case, they were to be sequestered. The selection process had taken a week, and there were some problems. One prospective member said he was convinced that Cherry was mentally incompetent to stand trial. One man had the same last name as Cherry but told the judge he was not a relative. But what was strange, the man said, was that he had received a telephone call from someone who spoke of the trial. The judge asked the FBI to look into the caller's intent. The prospective juror said he would not have been concerned except for the fact that the call was made at 1:18 A.M.

And even after trial started there was a snag. One of the sixteen, an executive with a Birmingham company, told the judge that a major business transaction had blossomed that very week and he felt he needed to be on the job. The judge asked if that deal would distract him from listening to the evidence. "Obviously it would," the juror replied. "That's why I brought it up." He was excused. In the end, there were six white men, three white women, and three black men.

There were so many preliminary hearings and motions in the case that court reporter Julia W. Carter would ultimately fill up twenty-four volumes with testimony and other proceedings.

40

Cherry came to court wearing a dark suit, blue shirt, and dark tie. He wore a lapel pin of the American flag. He sat on the left side of his attorneys, Mickey Johnson and Rodger Bass. The latter told the news media that he was confident of acquittal, that the state did not have credible evidence, and that in fact the FBI had even lost large amounts of evidence collected at the church.

One of the spectators was Jack Neill, eighty, a veteran of World War II who had retired after a career in real estate. "I thought when it happened they should find the guys that did it and string 'em up," he told the author. "Those little girls hadn't done anything. The thing was horrible."

One of the first witnesses was Barbara Cross, daughter of the church's pastor, the Reverend John Cross. She was thirteen in 1963. Questioned by Jones, she told of the Youth Day service. "The lesson we talked about was what we do if somebody did something wrong against us, like punch us," she said. "And we would say the initials 'WWJD,' which means 'What Would Jesus Do.'" She said she was in a Sunday school class with Cynthia Wesley and Carole Robertson and the two had gone to the women's lounge after the class ended. She said the explosion occurred a short time later.

Mrs. Alpha Robertson testified of hurrying to the church and the dread she felt when she viewed the rubble.

"Did Carole have a Bible with her that day?" Jones asked.

"Yes, she had a Bible with her that day," she said. "And

I have that Bible now. From the rubbish came her Bible and wallet and billfold with pictures of school."

Another witness was Jimmy Parker, who attended Phillips High School in 1957. He worked for educational television at the time, he said. He said one day in September of 1957 he went to the school to pick up a transcript of his records; as he was leaving he saw a crowd of whites attacking a few blacks, including Fred Shuttlesworth. Parker said he grabbed his camera and began filming. He said there were about fifty white people in all, but most of the violence was by only a few. The main one was a man with a cigarette in his mouth.

Another witness, Bobby Birdwell, who was twelve in 1963, testified that he had played with one of Cherry's sons during that time. He said he saw Cherry in a KKK robe. Cochran showed him the film of the Shuttlesworth beating and asked if he recognized anyone. He pointed to the man with a cigarette in his mouth. It was Cherry. Birdwell also testified that he had been at the Cherry house one day in September of 1963 and several men were in the kitchen talking. He heard them use the word "bomb" and mention the Sixteenth Street Church.

Dr. Robert Brissie, the coroner, testified that he examined photos of the four girls and could tell by the extent of injury to each that death was a result of the explosion, which hurled debris.

Cochran asked, "Dr. Brissie, can I get you to . . . you to talk about blast waves . . . how it is that a blast kills a human being?"

"Well, when you have a high-order explosion . . . you have numerous fragments, pieces of wood, stone, brickbats . . . you get projectiles," Brissie said. "If these strike an individual, they may pass through. They may, they may even decapitate."

Retired FBI agent Richard Killion testified that he and agent Robert Zimmers arrived in Birmingham that afternoon and examined the bombed church. Posey asked what his impressions were at the scene.

"I concluded that it was not accidental," Killion said. "It was a high-order explosion, which means the velocity is much more . . . bricks were blown into small pieces."

In cross-examination by Johnson, the retired agent was asked if a natural gas explosion would produce the same kind of damage.

"A gas explosion can knock down walls," Killion said, "but it does not tend to fragment materials." The church explosion, he stressed, resulted from dynamite or a military explosive. Then he added, "It was a high-order explosion, and when it occurs, it will be at the rate of 16,000 to 22,000 feet a second, which provides the velocity" to turn debris into deadly missiles.

Richard Harris, who was retired from Alabama Gas Company, testified, as he did in the Blanton trial, that the explosion at the church was not the result of a gas leak.

While the FBI did not have as many tapes of Cherry as they did of Blanton, there were still a number of comments captured that would have a damaging impact on the defendant. Both the Burns tapes and those taken at the Blanton kitchen would play a key role.

Retired FBI agent Ralph Butler testified about putting the tapes in the trunk of Burns's car and then taking them out when Burns returned from an evening cruising around Birmingham with Blanton. One tape contained comments from Cherry.

Johnson, on cross-examination, asked Butler if he ever observed Burns being drunk when he returned.

"I just got the tapes, I never observed his behavior," Butler said. "I just got the tapes out. I'd say something like 'Glad you're back,' or something like that."

When Ben Herren was called to testify, the attorneys adjourned to Garrett's office to argue over the admissibility of certain aspects of the recordings.

Cochran told Garrett that the conversation showed a conspiracy. He pointed out a part where Cherry says, "The FBI gave me a polygraph and I lied all the way through it."

"He laughs about it," Cochran said. "That is what conspirators do. They throw curve balls at the FBI and laugh about it. The tape shows just by the conversation . . . the joking about the 'N' word . . . I mean there is clearly a familiarity here. They are talking about the Klan, about who in the Klan they can trust. They are talking about 'niggers.' These are racists who are Klan buddies."

Johnson rebutted the argument by saying that Burns once asked Blanton if Cherry was a friend of his. Blanton's response was confusing: "I don't know if Cherry knows anything at all."

But Garrett allowed a portion of the tapes to be played for the jury. It starts off with a siren being heard in the distance, and Cherry and Blanton joke about "where were you guys when the church blew up?" There is laughter. Then Cherry says, "Yeah. We're just trying to make a bomb. We ain't got ours made yet."

Cherry adds, "I was a demolition expert in the Marine Corps." Later there is a conversation about some bombs being found in Birmingham that had not exploded. And Cherry says, "They said they had the wrong kind of caps on two of them."

"What kind of batteries do they use?" asks Blanton.

"Hell, I don't know what kind they used," replies Cherry. "Hell, a flashlight battery would have set it off. Hell, they have had it in there when a clock, the alarm, or something . . . the mother-fucker makes contact, you see."

On a tape recorded March 29, 1965, Cherry is heard saying, "The FBI came here and I didn't tell them shit." Later he said, "The FBI thinks the bomb was made somewhere else," and then he is heard laughing.

Blanton cautions, "Careful what you say around this boy," meaning Burns. "He doesn't know too much. Let's keep it that way."

Prosecutors were able to introduce into evidence a number of interviews conducted by FBI agents with Cherry in 1963 and 1964. In one, he said he had quit the KKK in August of 1963 "because I was against violence." To which

Cochran, in an aside, remarked, "That must have been news to Fred Shuttlesworth." In a second interview with the FBI, Cherry changes his story and says he had rejoined the KKK after the bombing. At a third interview, he told the FBI he had quit in January 1963. In a September 1964 interview he told an agent, "The only reason I didn't do the church bombing was, maybe, because somebody beat me to it." Another document signed by Cherry states that on the night of September 13 he was at Merle Snow's Modern Sign Company helping make signs to protest integration. He says he was there from about 7 P.M. until midnight.

In a later interview with the author, Cochran recalled:

> We had to get the jury to get an idea of what Cherry was like back in 1963. Here they were looking at the old grandfather sitting there, and we needed to show that he wasn't always that way. We had the people saying things that he said twenty years after the fact, but sometimes an ex-wife or other family member isn't always a great witness. I knew we needed to find something from Cherry that went back to 1963, the time of the bombing. And we found this written statement, in his own handwriting, that he had given the FBI back in 1963 that said he had been at the Modern Sign Company the night of September 13, the Friday before the bombing. So we had that, then we had Tommy Blanton's kitchen tapes where he said he had been at the Modern Sign Company making the bomb—you know, the big meeting where they made the bomb or planned the bomb. So we were able to tie those together, and Judge Garrett allowed us to play the tape because we showed that there was this conspiracy to conceal evidence about the bombing.

Posey called Willadean Brogdon, who had once been married to the defendant. She took the witness stand, explaining to the judge, "I have restless legs syndrome, and may have to take some medicine."

She testified that she had been a truck driver when she met Cherry in early 1970. She told of their meeting at truck stops. In August of 1970 they were married, she said, but the marriage ended in divorce in April of 1973. She said she was afraid of Cherry.

Posey asked if she had seen Cherry with any KKK attire.

"I saw a Ku Klux Klan robe in a footlocker," she said. "It was red-striped and had some gold on the shoulders."

Asked if he ever mentioned the church, she replied:

"Once he broke down and pointed at the church. We were riding through Birmingham. He pointed at the church and said that was where he put the bomb down. He said he lit the fuse. He said he regretted that children were killed, but at least they wouldn't grow up to have more niggers. Those were his words."

Later she added, "He said he was Robert Shelton's right-hand man." Shelton had been the imperial wizard of the United Klans of America.

"Did you see the red robe?" Posey asked.

Brogdon nodded. "He put it on and danced all around, to show what he looked like as a Klan person."

She said that when they separated, Cherry called her to meet him in Mt. Olive, just north of Birmingham. She said she went there, stopped the car, and waited as he came to the window to talk. Then she floored it, she said. "I put my foot on the gas and took off," she said.

"Did you look back?" Posey asked.

"I didn't."

Under cross-examination by Johnson, Brogdon testified that she had once lost custody of her children, but later regained it. She was also charged with kidnapping, a charge she said was dismissed.

Questioning her about the dates of her marriage to Cherry and the divorce, Johnson found some inconsistencies. Once she had said they were married in April of 1970, another time it was June. The divorce was in April of 1973 on one telling, but under further questioning that month changed. She obviously became confused about some of the dates. At one point she prompted him in an irritated tone, "You should write some of this down."

Later she repeated that Cherry had told her about placing the bomb at the church the night before the explosion and making the statement "I lit the fuse." Then she added, "Sometimes he cried."

"You didn't say anything about Bobby crying to the grand jury," Johnson declared.

Brogdon said she called the FBI in Montana when she heard news accounts that the case was being reopened. She talked to agents in 1999. She said she thought he had been in prison, and had never attempted to contact him. "I didn't want to hear about him," she said.

Judge Garrett interrupted court for a few minutes to allow students from Gordon School in East Providence, Rhode Island, to enter the courtroom and find seats. He announced that teachers were leading a group visiting Birmingham and wanted to sit in on the trial for a while. Lynn Bowman, the teacher of the eighth graders, said, "As a history teacher, you want to personalize history . . . you can't get closer than this." Student Abby Waite, fourteen, said, "It's definitely history."

The students heard witness Charley Wayne Brogdon, a brother of Willadean Brogdon, testify.

Questioned by Cochran, he testified that Cherry once showed him a KKK robe and talked of racial issues.

"What did you talk about?" Cochran asked.

"Race. The Klan. He used the 'N' word."

"Anything else?"

Brogdon, a short, husky man with a butch haircut, nodded. "He told me he made the bomb, the one that killed four kids in the church." Later he added, "He was remorseful some of the time, then hateful."

Defense attorney Johnson cross-examined, moving quickly to what was said about a bomb.

"Did he tell you he lit the fuse to the bomb?"

"No," Brogdon replied. "He just said he built the bomb."

"Did you ask him any questions?"

"No."

Brogdon, who had spent some time in prison, said he had told his probation officer about Cherry and the bomb.

"What did he say?" Johnson asked.

"Said stay away from him."

Another witness who made contact with the FBI was a granddaughter of the defendant, Teresa Stacey. She said she had called in 1997 when she saw Cherry at a news conference denying that he had bombed the church. She testified that when she was ten years old she heard him say, "I helped blow up a bunch of niggers back in Birmingham."

Then Michael Wayne Gowins, who was in his sixties, was called. He came into the courtroom in a wheelchair and had an oxygen tank attached. He once lived in Birmingham, he testified, then moved to Texas, later returning to Alabama. Questioned by Cochran, he testified that in the early 1980s he managed some apartments in the Dallas area. They were owned by his mother. He said one day the carpets were to be cleaned, and the man who did the cleaning was Bobby Frank Cherry. "We all had a Birmingham connection," he said.

"What was being said?" Cochran asked.

"Well, he and my mother were talking about Mexicans coming into America, and he said something about them leaving apartments dirty," Gowins said.

"Anything else?"

"Yes, he said he had to get out of Birmingham, because of the blacks," Gowins said. "He said, 'The niggers were taking over.'"

"Anything else?"

"About the Klan," Gowins said.

"He said he was in the Klan?"

"Yeah, and he said, 'You know, I bombed that church,'" Gowins said. "Well, at that time it got real quiet. And about that time he got through working and left."

The words, spoken matter-of-factly, hung over the courtroom. Then Cochran asked when Gowins decided to tell someone about it.

"About ten years later, I read where the FBI was looking for the church bombers and I called them, the FBI," he said. "I told them he was out there saying he had bombed it."

Under cross-examination by Johnson, Gowins said he had never known Cherry in Birmingham. Johnson suggested Gowins had an ulterior motive for calling the FBI.

"All this came up," he said, "after Bobby Cherry sued your mother, isn't that right?"

"No, he didn't have to sue my mother." Johnson then moved on, dropping the issue.

Tommy Blanton's ex-wife, Jean Casey, was called to the witness stand and questioned by Cochran. She had remarried, and her last name was now Barnes. He asked her about the night of September 13, 1963, the night Blanton had stood her up. She remembered, she said, that she had wondered where he was. "I called the Modern Sign Company," she said. "Somebody said he wasn't there." But, she testified, Blanton told her later that he was at the sign shop. That's when he made the reference, captured on tape, to making a bomb. The connection would be tied to Cherry's alleged involvement.

George Ferris of Union City, California, a nephew of Willadean Brogdon, testified that Cherry had once asked him about joining the KKK, but that he refused.

"He ever make comments about blacks?" Cochran asked.

"Just that he hated, hated niggers."

"Any comment about bombings?"

Ferris nodded. "He said that damn church should have been full of niggers."

Blanton (*left*) and Cherry, in jailhouse garb, at their initial hearing after being indicted. (Courtesy *The Birmingham News*)

Doug Jones speaks to reporters after the Blanton verdict. From left, agent Ben Herren, Assistant U.S. Attorney Robert Posey, and Jefferson County Assistant District Attorney Jeff Wallace. Agent Bill Fleming is partly visible at rear. (Courtesy *The Birmingham News*)

Retired FBI Special-Agent-In-Charge of the Birmingham office Rob Langford, who reopened the case in 1995. (Photo by Frank Sikora)

A group carries a large photo of Virgil Ware, the teen who was shot to death as he rode his bike on the day of the bombing. He was reinterred in 2004. (Photo by Frank Sikora)

Assistant U.S. Attorney Don Cochran took a leading role in the Cherry case. (Photo by Frank Sikora)

Bill Fleming, the FBI agent who, with Herren, spearheaded the investigation of Cherry and Blanton. (Photo by Frank Sikora)

41

On May 20 the defense began presentation of its case. Defense attorneys Johnson and Bass opted not to put Cherry on the stand, but they did call witnesses to try to offset the damaging testimony put on by the state.

Among the first to testify was Mary Frances Cunningham, who stated to the FBI on December 7, 1964, that she and another woman—either Flora Lee Chambliss or Elizabeth Cobbs—had driven to the church late on the night of September 14–15, 1963, and observed Blanton's car. In that statement, she said Cherry got out and walked down the alley carrying a satchel. Chambliss was there, and another man later identified as Herman Frank Cash. Years later, when the account came to public attention, she recanted. Now, Johnson and Bass maintained that the entire government case against Cherry (and earlier Blanton) was based on this fabricated story. Called to the stand on a Saturday morning, Mrs. Cunningham, in her mid-seventies, denied knowing anything at all about such an incident or making any statement.

Prosecutors did not ask any questions. Bob Eddy was called to the stand and testified that in 1977 he had heard the account from Cunningham—then known as Gail Tarrant—but said that later she denied it.

Called to the stand again was Bill Jackson, a barber who had associated with Klan members for a short time in 1963. Jackson had been a witness for the state in both the Cham-

244

bliss and Blanton cases, but in this one he was called as a witness for the defense.

Johnson did the questioning. Jackson testified about events in 1963, saying he had been introduced to Blanton and to Chambliss, both KKK members. He then testified about the day the three of them and others gathered at the Cahaba River bridge on U.S. 280 southeast of Birmingham. He said about fifteen people attended and the purpose was recruitment, to start a new klavern.

Then Johnson moved to the night of September 13, 1963. "Did you go to the Modern Sign Shop?"

"Yes, sir." Jackson replied, saying it was about 7 P.M.

"And what took place there?"

"Well, they were making Confederate flags and signs."

"What was the purpose of this? What were they to be used for?"

"To be used in parades. There was a lot going on."

He was referring to the demonstrations by whites protesting the desegregation of West End High School.

Johnson asked if he saw Blanton and Chambliss at the sign shop.

"Yes. I remember Tommy rambling around in the trunk."

He said the two left together in Blanton's 1957 Chevrolet.

"You know Bobby Frank Cherry?" Johnson asked.

"No, sir," Jackson answered.

"When was the first time you saw Bobby Frank Cherry?" Johnson asked.

Jackson looked at Cherry. "I met him for the first time this morning."

On cross-examination, Cochran basically used the same tactic that the defense had used with Jackson in the Blanton trial—that he had lied.

"Mr. Jackson," Cochran said, "you were a klansman, that's right?"

"No, sir," he said. "Never been."

"Just on a fact-finding mission about the Klan?"

Jackson nodded. "I did some fact-finding."

"Writing a school paper on it or something?" Cochran quizzed.

"No, sir. I'm just interested."

"Isn't it in fact true that you lied to the FBI, Mr. Jackson?" Cochran asked.

"I lied to the FBI once in a jailhouse," the witness responded. "I told them I didn't know Tommy Blanton."

Two of the defendant's grandsons, Glenn Belcher and Bobby Wayne Cherry, both in their twenties, testified that they had never heard Cherry say he bombed a church. They said he referred to African Americans as "Negroes."

Robert High, forty-six, the pastor of a small church in Mabank, Texas, said Cherry attended services three times a month. The congregation, he said, was about half black and half white. He said Cherry mingled well.

Asked by Johnson if he ever heard Cherry use the "N" word, High blithely replied, "Yes, I have."

"Often?" Johnson asked.

"Well, yeah." Then High added that he had used it himself. His effort to explain that he said it when he was younger was cut off by an objection from Jones.

Johnson and Bass had planned to use Eddie Mauldin as a witness, but the retired hotel worker had died a few months after the Blanton trial. With the state's agreement, Johnson was allowed to read Mauldin's testimony from the Blanton trial into the record.

Mauldin had stated that, moments before the explosion, he was standing about a block from the church when he noticed a Rambler station wagon drive by with two Confederate flags flying on the front. He said there were two young white men in it. When the bomb detonated, he said, the car "burned rubber" as it sped away.

A reluctant defense witness was Carolyn McKinstry, who was fifteen in 1963. She was a member of the church and made a statement to the FBI on the day of the bombing, saying she heard a telephone ring in a little office behind the altar. She answered and heard a man say, "The bomb will go off in three minutes." She said she went into the sanctuary and at that moment heard the explosion. The evening before she was to testify, she called Johnson and said she did not want to take the stand and had a doctor's appointment in the morning. Given this information, Judge Garrett advised the attorneys to get her into court and bring the doctor if necessary.

She took the stand and repeated the statement about the phone call. Johnson's intention was clear: If someone called with precise timing for when the bomb would go off, it would offset the FBI's position that the type of bomb and the igniting device were unknown.

42

————
————
————

In his closing, Cochran told the jurors that the four girls were "just the absolute picture of innocence," but the bombing had swept their lives away, changing forever the worlds of their families. "Ladies and gentlemen . . . for almost thirty-nine years this defendant had avoided justice. In fact, the evidence shows that for almost thirty-nine years this defendant has mocked justice. Ladies and gentlemen, the time for justice is here. Now Mr. Johnson has tried from the start of this case . . . [to] have you believe that this investigation started on the seventh of December 1964, because a statement given by Mary Frances Cunningham caused this investigation to jump off on a side track, and ever since that moment they have wrongly accused this man. In fact, what the evidence shows is that this defendant was a prime suspect from the start. By my count, he was interviewed at least ten times by the FBI before December the seventh, 1964."

Cochran paused, then told the jury members that only one investigation really mattered in the case—the one they would begin in their deliberations. He told them to rely on common sense.

"Now, you're not going to know everything that happened in Birmingham about this bombing back in September of 1963. Juries never know everything. And certainly [with] a case tried this long after it happened, you're not going to know everything. But you will know enough.

You'll know enough to know that this defendant is guilty. Whoever took a bomb on Saturday night, or Sunday morning . . . and put it underneath those concrete steps next to the Sixteenth Street Baptist Church, a bomb that was so big and so powerful that those steps simply ceased to exist . . . to put that next to a house of God, a house of worship . . . on a Sunday morning, if that doesn't show an utter disregard for human life, than I don't know what does."

Cochran spoke of Cherry's penchant for violence in the 1950s and 1960s, the beating of Fred Shuttlesworth, the striking of a black person in a restaurant. Cherry, he said, "not only talked about violence. As they say today, he walked the walk."

Then he talked about the motive for a bombing of the church.

"Well, motive, you always have to sort of think of [it] in a common-sense way. I suppose, I suppose it could be a coincidence that the biggest, the deadliest, the worst bomb of all of the bombs in Birmingham just happened to happen five days after the public schools were integrated for the first time. That could be a coincidence, I suppose. But your common sense tells you otherwise. That the timing of this bomb immediately after the first time that public schools are integrated tells you, by common sense, what probably was the motive for this."

Cochran cited a statement Cherry made in 1963 to the FBI that he hated school integration, that he wished black attorney Arthur Shores had been killed when his house was bombed, and that "the only reason I didn't do the church bombing was that somebody beat me to it." He pointed out that the Blanton tapes had said "we" met at the Modern Sign Company to "make the bomb." And then he said Cherry had given a statement to the FBI in 1963 that he had been at the small sign shop just three blocks away from the church. Aiding and abetting, Cochran repeated.

Cochran continued, "It makes perfect sense that if you're going to arm the biggest bomb that's been used in Birmingham, that you're going to do it somewhere close to the church. Maybe they built the fuse at his [Cherry's] house and finally put the thing together and armed the fuse there at the Modern Sign Company. They only had to go three blocks to get it to the church. All they had to do was leave it there on Friday night, come back and pick it up on Saturday and drop it off."

He concluded by saying that Cherry and his KKK cohorts took away the young lives because of their hatred. He showed pictures of the girls on the video screen. The last was Denise McNair, who was eleven, shown hugging her Chatty Cathy doll. Said Cochran, "She never got to be fourteen years old. Never got to get over being so naive that she didn't even understand that she was supposed to hate that doll because it had different colored skin than she did. Ladies and gentlemen, the time for justice is here. In fact, it's way overdue."

In the closing for the defense, Johnson attacked the character of some of the witnesses, especially Willadean Brogdon. He also hammered home his opinion that the prosecutors had based their case on the story told by Mary Frances Cunningham, even though she had later denied it. No evidence tied Cherry to the bombing, he said, only speculation and uncorroborated statements, made years after the bombing.

"It seems strange," he said, speaking of Mrs. Cunningham, "that the men the FBI go after are the same ones she names. She told the story back in 1964, but no one in Washington took note because they probably thought it sounded a little phony. Somebody comes up after a year and says 'I was there.' And you want to go to that person and say, 'Why in hell didn't you say something to save lives?'"

Johnson said the deaths of the four girls was the result of hatred that the state had allowed to persist during the 1960s. "The memories of those children will survive anything we do here," he said. "And they will always be cherished. And they will always be important because of what—because of the change that they have made in all of us. Nothing we can do here can add anything to the importance of their memories." But, he added, to convict a man who had not been proven guilty would not serve justice.

Doug Jones came forward with his closing statement. The bombing, he said, "was a shock wave of shame" for Birmingham. "This was the most heinous of crimes, an attack on God's house, where innocent children were preparing to conduct the first of monthly youth worship services. And it rippled through the world where good and decent people asked why. Is nothing sacred in Birmingham, Alabama, where innocent children cannot even go and worship without fear of death or injury?"

But, he added, Bobby Frank Cherry "wore the shock like a badge of honor, a KKK badge of honor," adding that the men who hid under their hoods were the "forefathers of terrorism." He showed again the picture of Denise McNair holding her doll. "It is an image of hope," he told the jurors, "the dream that all God's children can live together. In 1963 it was the hope of a race of people. Today it is the hope of all of us." Cherry, he said, was blinded by hate and wanted to destroy that hope. "He simply could not understand that hope is a good thing, and good things never die. I ask you to hold this defendant accountable . . . and when you do . . . justice will truly roll down like a mighty river."

The jury deliberated one afternoon, then retired for the night at the hotel. Cochran recalls that he didn't sleep well that night, worrying about the case. It had not been an easy case to try. The jury resumed deliberations in the morning. Sherie Mayfield, forty-seven, a teacher and member of the jury, later told of the calculating process of deciding Cherry's fate. "We didn't vote at first, but started from the beginning," she said. "We put everything in a category. We had a blackboard and we put things in there and we discussed them all: tying Cherry to the KKK; the identification of Cherry beating Reverend Shuttlesworth; Willadean Brogdon and what Cherry had told her. We put it all together and the pieces fit. I was impressed with the testimony of Mitch Burns, Bobby Birdwell, and Willadean Brogdon. We voted once, on the second day of deliberation. It was 12:30 when we took that first vote. We wrote it on a piece of paper, either guilty or not guilty. And the young lady who was the foreperson read out the results. They were all guilty. Then at 12:50 we took a vote on whether it was first-degree or second-degree murder, and the result was again unanimous—first-degree murder. I remember my stomach was queasy. And we knocked on the door and the deputy—we called him 'Cream Puff' because he was so big and tough— came to the door and we told him. He got all excited, because he had to find everyone as most were still at lunch."

Mayfield said she had observed Cherry during the trial, as he sat staring at nothing, barely looking at witnesses; it made her wonder about his mental state. But during a break outside, she noticed him smoking a cigarette and talking to his attorneys. "He was very animated," she said.

At about 1:30, the attorneys and spectators were in their seats. The judge asked that the verdict be read. Cherry and his attorney rose and faced the jury. The verdict was guilty of four counts of murder. Cherry winced slightly as he turned toward Johnson. Bass patted him on the shoulder. Then Judge Garrett asked him if he had anything to say.

"Yeah. The whole bunch has lied all the way through this thing," he said, pointing at the prosecution table. "Doug Jones. That punk there. And that bird there. The whole bunch has lied all the way through. And I told the truth. And I don't know why I'm going to jail for nothing. I haven't done anything."

The sentence was life in prison. There was not an outpouring of elation after the decision. As Cherry was led away, members of the girls' families hugged each other. Those in Cherry's family sat silently, some of them weeping. One young man clutched a Bible.

Junie Collins Peavy, a sister of Addie Mae Collins, sat in the front row, staring ahead. When asked how she felt, she responded wearily, "We just want it to come to an end. It's been so many years."

And her sister, Sarah Collins Rudolph, the only survivor in the lounge on that horrific day in 1963, lamented, "It's about to drive me crazy. It has caused so much pain for me. But if they found someone else to prosecute, I'd come back and testify again."

Anne Driver, who had run to the church and saw the bodies being removed from the debris, thought about the verdict and the bombing. "I can't describe how I felt. You didn't know how to react." She paused, gathering her thoughts, then added: "The girls would be relieved that justice has been done."

After so many years, it had been done, finally.

Bill Fleming would later draw his own conclusions about the case: "I don't think they intended to kill anyone. You know, if James Lay hadn't seen those two guys that night a couple of weeks earlier, and they had put a bomb down then, it would have gone off early on a Tuesday morning and probably no one would have been hurt. And that might have been it." It was a point of view that many lawmen held. But Robert Posey held another view.

> You know, we thought about that a lot. But at the time there was great unrest and demonstrations about school integration. Then, on the tenth day of September, 1963, the schools were integrated. U.S. marshals were brought in and it was done. Well, that whole week there was a banner on the church saying that Sunday was going to be "Youth Day." So when you put those things together, you wonder. We may never know exactly what happened at the Modern Sign Shop on the nights of the thirteenth and fourteenth, but it was clear that these individuals were there, and the focus of events was centered around that shop.

Doug Jones says simply, "The convictions we got in 2001 and 2002 should have happened thirty-seven years earlier."

Some of those who had been at the center of the case did not live long after Cherry's conviction. Mitch Burns, the former klansman who had tape-recorded both Blanton and Cherry for the FBI, died in November of 2002. Alpha

Robertson passed away shortly after, as did Michael Gowins. And defense attorney Rodger Bass died within a year of Cherry's conviction, at age forty. Bass, who had served six years in the Army, was deeply troubled by the verdict. His death was ruled an accidental overdose, according to the Shelby County coroner, Doug Ballard.

In the spring of 2004, a seminar on civil rights cases in Alabama and Mississippi was held at Birmingham-Southern College. It was called "The Gathering." The attorneys who prosecuted, the investigators who probed the cases, and the families of the victims all took part. It was an auspicious event. Bill Baxley, whose efforts in the early 1970s had started it all, summed it up this way: "Justice was delayed . . . but justice was not denied."

Postscript

In his closing argument in the Cherry case, Doug Jones told the jury that Denise McNair's grave was just a short distance from the downtown. I had visited Shadow Lawn Cemetery years before—her grave is on a little rise and is overlooked by a pine tree—and on that day, a restless wind had hummed through the boughs.

Carole Robertson, Cynthia Wesley and Addie Mae Collins are at Woodland Cemetery (also known as Greenland Cemetery) in the eastern part of Birmingham, near the airport. For many years Addie's grave was unmarked. One of the Collins sisters told me she had gone there and could not find where Addie was buried. In the 1990s a group of citizens raised money to place a marker in her memory. However, no one could find the exact site where she was buried.

Over the years death had claimed Mr. and Mrs. Collins, the Wesleys, and the Robertsons. Bobby Frank Cherry, diagnosed with cancer, died on November 18, 2004 at a prison hospital.

In 2004, Virgil Ware, the thirteen-year-old youth shot to death as he rode his bicycle that Sunday, was removed from an overgrown plot at Pratt City, a Birmingham suburb, and re-interred on a slope at the George Washington Carver Memorial Gardens.

The inscription on Denise McNair's white stone marker sums up that terrible day in Birmingham. It reads:

Carol Denise McNair
   November 17, 1951
   September 15, 1963
She loved all—but a mad bomber hated her kind.

In his closing argument, Jones had spoken of the words on the grave. And he said that, at last, justice had rolled down.

Index

Index

Index

Index

Index

Index

Index

Index

Index

Index